Summary

these hot afternoons "it's quite absurd"
sunlight stirring her cotton dress inside , ̲̲̲̲̲̲̲̲̲̲̲̲ ̲̲̲̲̲ ̲̲̲̲̲̲
an afternoon room crashed not breaking a bone or flower.
a list of cities crumbled under riots and distant gun-fire
yet the stone buildings sparkle. It is not only
the artificial lakes in the parks . . . perhaps . . .
but various illusions of belonging fall with equal noise and regularity
how could they know, the office girls as well
"fancy falling for him . . ." and inherit a sickness
such legs fat and voluptuous . . . smiling to himself
the length of train journeys

the whole landscape of suburban railway tracks,
passive canals and coloured oil-refineries.
it could be worse—

at intervals messages got through
the senate was deserted all that summer
black unmarked airplanes would suddenly appear
and then leave the sky surprised at its quiet
"couldn't you bear my tongue in your mouth?"

skin so smooth in the golden half-light
I work through nervousness to a poor but
convincing appearance of bravery and independence

mexico crossed by railways. aztec ruins
finally demolished and used for spanning one more ravine
in a chain of mountain tunnels and viaducts
and not one tear to span her grief
to lick him in the final mad-house hysteria
of armour falling off, rivets flying in all directions like fire-crackers,
and the limp joy of the great break-down
which answers so many questions.
a series of lovers—but could you?—
all leading through the same door after the first hours

of confused ecstasies.
the dream woman who eats her lover.
would suffocation be an exaggeration of what really happens?
the man who forgets, leaving the shop
without his parcels, but meaning no harm.
"it's all a question of possession,
jealousy and . . ." the ability to torment,
the subtle bullying of night long talkings.
what artificial fruits can compare with this
and the wrecked potting-sheds that lie open
throughout the land? gorging their misery
and that of others . . . geranium flowers hacked off the plants
by gentlemen's canes and now limp on the gravel
    paths wandering through empty lawns and shrubberies
afternoon bickerings on a quiet park bench while
families take tea at a convenient cafe, so nicely situated.

engines and greased axles clattering through the shunting-yards.
fluttering parasols running for cover
under the nearby elms as the first heavy sweet raindrops
lick the girls forehead. the slightly hysterical
conversations crowded beneath the leaking branches
waiting for the july thunder to pass. The damp heat
and discomfort of clothes, a tongue passing the length
of her clitoris . . . and back again . . .
erections in the musty pavilion which should lead to a lake
but doesn't. the resin scent and dry throat in the pine wood
across the meadows.
               "surely you remember?"
but so long ago.

strawberries lining her lake in the dark woods
an old picture slowly fading on the wall
as if a flower too could change her face
as a dusk cloaks our loneliness

Lee Harwood in Rotherhithe Tunnel, 1964.

INTERVIEW 1 — SEPTEMBER 2007

When the ricks were burnt

KC My simple idea is that we start at the beginning of your work and take a walk through it and talk about things as we go along. I've sent you some questions and you've not crushed them into a ball and thrown them back at me! We'll assume we can go with the questions. I was looking for a poem that was distinctive of that time, very near the beginning of your writing. Can we talk about the poem 'Summer'? Is it typical of your early work?

LH Yes, I think it may be. With those poems in *The Man With Blue Eyes*, there are quite a few direct lyric, love poems, though they are not especially direct. There is a lot of collage in them. 'Summer' isn't part of that sequence of love poems but it is part of that period and that approach to writing.

KC Can you remember writing the poem 'Summer'?

LH No.

KC What were you thinking about?

LH I don't know.

KC What were you thinking?

LH It's so long ago, I really can't remember but because of you mentioning it I read it again. I can see various incidents, things that happened, not just that particular summer but over a few summers, all came together in that poem. It's really a bundle of stories creating an atmosphere. It's also the pleasure, for me, of picking up a story and running with it, seeing where it will go, like a runaway horse. It was a recognition of what writing could do.

KC Heady times.

LH Yes. You can have a pattern of behaviour which, when you
    recognise it, you have the choice of continuing or to move into
    a new territory. Meeting and spending time with John Ashbery
    in 1965 gave me the choice to move into a whole new approach
    to writing. If not totally new, a more satisfying approach. It was
    not that John was talking about writing to me, it was just odd
    remarks that clicked and made me recognise what I could do, and
    what I had been doing until then. He wasn't really interested in
    writing about himself—most people's personal lives are boring
    he said. He was interested in writing about almost a shared life,
    like the life of dreams, the sort of shared material we can all
    enter. Later on I realised this was akin to various works of art
    that I like. Such as Cornell's boxes or the unfinished paintings
    of Gustave Moreau. You're presented with a scene and invited
    to walk in and wander around, like entering a toy theatre, and
    you can create things to entertain yourself and possibly a reader.
    The idea of constructing poems that did this seemed wonderful.
    Poems like Ashbery's 'Europe' and 'How much longer will I be
    able to inhabit the divine sepulcher' are marvellous examples of
    this building with fragments and suggestions.

        I realised then that while Ashbery had triggered this
    realisation, it had already been building up, like a chemical build
    up. A taste for this had begun in 1962 when I read Jorge Luis
    Borges' *Ficciones*. Most of Borges' pieces are only a few pages
    long but completely take you into their world. It isn't just about
    Argentinian culture. It could be set in ancient history or 19th
    century France. It's a whole fascinating world beyond your
    own life. Reading those stories, where often enough the rug is
    pulled out from under the reader's feet, is so exciting, such fun.
    Even earlier, around 1959/1960 I'd become interested in Tristan
    Tzara's poetry and his Dada activities. He collages material and
    it's more fragmented than Borges and Ashbery, but it has the

same principle. So the taste, the curiosity was there, but Ashbery was the one who sparked me to put it into action.

KC And this helped create a poetry unusual for the local climate. It wasn't a poetry in which somebody is bleating out their happy or sad heart in English quatrains?

LH Not that they are doing harm or frightening the horses but I wanted something else, something which was exciting and pulled the reader in and was more demanding. It wasn't telling a story in a straightforward way. It was telling a story, but not the "look at me, I'm suffering" or "look at me, this, that and the other."

KC The poems 'Summer' and 'The man with blue eyes' are in that first style.

LH Yes—the stuff before that was indistinguishable from what was churned out in London in the early 60s.

KC 'Summer' seems to me typical in that it is very charged—I can't tell you what the feelings are but it seems charged.

LH Looking at it again, which is very strange 42 years later, I can see that there is an intensity there and there are quite a few tussles going on. You've got these little intense scenes shifting round and you've got a parallel world which is benevolent. Dreadful things or loony things are happening elsewhere. You do get these moments of goodness, whether it be in some of the pastoral scenes or a landscape of suburban railway tracks and oil refineries. I guess that also ties in with some of the reading I'd been doing—Dada and early Surrealism, Reverdy's idea of *The Daily Miracle*—of how amazing all the things around you are when you look at them and step back rather than take them for granted. And so, there's that, which is quite positive, and this very intense story too with a lot of sexual experience in it.

KC So the sources and the feeling of the poem, neither are homogenised are they—there is a variance and a mixture all the way through?

LH Yes—and big jumps. About half way through the poem from what seems like a European setting suddenly you are in Mexico and with new railways being built using old Aztec masonry. The railways in themselves are exciting—beautiful structures, but built at a price. Then it moves back, I suppose, to Europe. That might seem a weird jolt not at all to do with the poem, but it has and I guess, because of being encouraged by reading Tzara, that's how its come out. Why not? Why should I take it out? I want this sort of poetics—to seem to use a whole world—like it's a paintbox . . .

KC You've just described the poetics of the early work, of what at the time you were aware of in your poetry and what was prompting you to write in that way?

LH I guess what I'm saying is bringing together these different elements. The landscape of emotional situations, and a story that is continually shifting—that's accurate.

KC In 'Summer' the lines are quite long. Here and in several of the poems of that time, the long lines generate sensuality as well as a sort of languor, it's relaxed but tense. Were you aware of that then? Do you agree with me? They are very physical poems, Lee. They are very involved with the body, aren't they?

LH Yes—there is the sexual side.

KC No—it's more diffuse than that do you think? It's certainly not for the Puritans.

LH Yes but with the long lines I think that's partly an echo of the idea of story telling, of how you said it's sensual, like being told a story. It's the most basic form of literature. It's why as children a thing we love most is being told a story. As you get older your stories get, in my case, more chopped up.

KC And the narrative draws the reader or the listener in doesn't it?

LH Yes, and the reason for the long lines is partly to signify that tone and also it's something I became more aware of from Ashbery. He would have long lines and when you would naturally think a line would end with one word, he would intentionally take that word and put it at the beginning of the next line. When you have a neat line ending where you expect it, it creates familiarity in the poem. By breaking the pattern and changing how the poem has to be read you jolt the reader, it makes them alert and so they pay more attention to the language as a whole.

KC It rearranges the thinking doesn't it?

LH Yes—and so they will be more alert, not being lulled by neat packages but trying to avoid anything neat.

KC There are elements of the poem which are sensual and languid and other formal elements which shake the reader, which takes the reader out of the pre-supposed way of reading. So there's quite a lot of push and pull in these poems isn't there?

LH Yes, so the poem is like a bundle of voices. The narrator, possibly the other people who would take over the job of the narration, because there is no one narrator, and at times the reader. There's one bit where it says, "'surely you remember?' / but so long ago." Is that someone talking to another in the poem or is that talking to the reader?

KC Who is talking and to whom is unfixed.

LH Yes, I mean there's that thing of *You*, when I've used the word *You* in a poem. I'm really not good at talking about this but I know someone who is! There is a very good interview with Ashbery.

KC OK—what is it he says?

LH This is a 1972 *New York Quarterly* interview—he says, "The personal pronouns in my work very often seem to be like variables in an equation. *You* can be myself or it can be another person, someone whom I'm addressing, and so can *he* and *she* for that matter and *we*. Sometimes one has to deduce from the rest of the sentence what is being meant, and my point is also that it doesn't really matter very much, that we are somehow all aspects of a consciousness giving rise to the poem and the fact of addressing someone, myself or someone else is what's the important thing at that particular moment, rather than the particular person involved, I guess. I don't have a very strong sense of my own identify and I find it very easy to move from one person in the sense of a pronoun to another and this again helps to produce a kind of polyphony in my poetry which I again feel is a means toward greater naturalism."

KC OK—I understand that, it sounds to me, I don't know, Frank O'Hara's Personism meets John Keats' negative capability. You're not convinced about what I've said I understand—no? What do you mean by not a strong sense of self—what do you think Ashbery means?

LH I just feel that a strong sense of self can be a hindrance. That it detracts from the relationship between the writer and the reader and it imposes the author's personality, and in a way that moves into the business of authority which I detest. I don't think any writing should be an authority rather than a questioning, otherwise it panders to the writer's vanity.

KC At the same time I do think it touches on negative capability . . .

LH I didn't say it didn't . . .

KC . . . an invisible self drawing upon others, which is what Keats means by it.

LH When I say that it's a hindrance, it is, but I can't deny that there's a human being writing this and equally, though I say pronouns are variable, it doesn't necessarily mean I'm not in there somewhere, for sure.

KC That takes me very neatly to my next question. You are writing a poetry that you have described to us in the mid 60s which in some ways is very not like the poetry that is immediately around it. It goes beyond the self, it's not impersonal but goes beyond autobiography. Somebody looking for autobiography in your poetry would come back with some mean pickings wouldn't they? However, we are interested in the autobiography and I know you were born in 1939—I don't know much after that. Just give us a potted version of the young Harwood. Where were you born?

LH I was born in passing in Leicester. My mother had gone to visit her family and I was about a month premature. I should have been born in Chertsey, Surrey. I was quickly hurried back there. I grew up in Chertsey on the Thames, it was a small country town then.

KC During the Second World War?

LH Yes. God this is such a vast subject. Basically, my childhood is, I suppose, what many people of my age and generation would have shared. You are born just before the War and your father goes off when you are about three or four months and, in my case, didn't come back until I was about six, because he was stationed so far away. And so I was brought up in a household with my mother and my grandmother. There was the London bombing and various houses nearby suddenly disappearing overnight. It's odd to say but it was a happy childhood despite this, except I didn't really have my father and my mother was working in a munitions factory so I didn't really see her much. Also my gran was a nurse so I was on my own quite a bit. But it seemed happy and I remember once when one of the rockets came over and landed in some fields about half a mile away it blew all the windows in and I slept through it and I woke up with the window frame on my bed and glass all over the floor and I still remember the sound of crunching glass as my mother came in the morning, picked me up out of bed and took me down stairs and I was really annoyed that I hadn't been woken up to see the rocket.

KC And you slept through it?

LH For some reason, yes—how bizarre.

KC And where did you go to school and what do you remember of school, Lee?

LH I remember a kind of kindergarten during the war.

KC Because your mother was at work?

LH Yes. She picked me up after she had finished her shift. I think I must have been the last kid to be picked up every day because other mums didn't appear to be working so late and I used to be sat on top of this bookcase by the window and there was a wooden clock to teach us how to tell the time. I would be just sitting there with this wooden clock, waiting. No, I don't want to get nostalgic about this time.

KC But as you say, the experience is typical of your generation..

LH Yes.

KC And that's why it's important.

LH We were okay, we had an allotment, we had vegetables. We got by and you didn't think you were deprived in any way.

KC I don't think it's nostalgia at all.

LH No, I think it's nostalgia—I just think it's boring people . . . I think the only sad legacy of it is that when I grew up and suddenly realised the horrors of this war, and especially what my father endured with the British Expeditionary Force at Dunkirk, and that by the time I was able to form the questions to ask how they managed that, how do they do it and how do they live with it afterwards, it was too late. He was dead and my mother had rewritten that history.

KC That's why it's important though. What you've just said is informative and it's there in your poetry as well, that attitude is there. That challenge to authority is there, isn't it?

LH Challenge to authority?

KC Oh I think so, to challenge whose history it is and who writes it.

LH Yes.

KC Yes, come on, in 'Bath-time', you know that poem 'Bath-time'— in *All The Wrong Notes*, what do you say? "The Cambridge Marxists, with large houses, cars and incomes can shove it." That's the challenge isn't it, who is laying claim to that history?

LH Yes.

KC So I rest my case. So, more childhood—growing up in the war— and then schools. What sort of schools did you go to?

LH When my father came back in 1946 we moved from garrison to garrison so I was in a series of different council schools and I think it must have thrown me somehow because I was very backward, I could hardly read and I ran away and stuff like that. So I was sent back to my grandmother's in Chertsey which equalled security for me in a way. I went to school there, and then I failed the 11+ but at that time the government was so desperate for an educated work force they had a 12+ as well. So I got in on a 12+ to a grammar school as a scholarship boy.

KC So you were an army brat?

LH Not really. My dad wasn't a professional soldier. He was a school teacher who taught maths before the war and again when he finally left the army. So I didn't belong to that network of military families and ex-pats and so on—I was never in that world. And my dad, when he left the military, never used his rank. He never talked about it, never talked to me about it ever.

KC Okay, so, school and then to university?

LH Yes, I went to Queen Mary College, University of London, which was ideal. It was mainly an engineering college with a smallish English department. I did a degree in English literature and language. I had this terrific thing of walking from Mile End tube or Stepney Green—I was living in Stepney anyway—to lectures and then coming out of the lecture and walking back along Mile End Road. So all that business of maybe going to a place like Cambridge where you would float out of your lectures in your gown and walk to the quad, and you could keep on living in that world was avoided. It was knocked out of you because you immediately had reality in your face and you didn't go to high table. You had bubble and squeak at the local transport café. I think that gave me a lovely sense of the importance of literature but also in the world, not in some isolated, privileged world. So you'd always have the measure of what you'd read, of the poetry existing in a working society.

KC And what was the teaching like? What were the lecturers like?

LH Most of them were pretty good, but there were some who just went by the book. There were a couple, one was Miss Thompson, who was an expert on the Elizabethan lyric and the other was a Dr Timmer, who taught Old English, and they were outstanding. They were just everything a scholar should be because they were always open. I would dot my essays with references to Dada and so on and Miss Thompson would ask me to a tutorial with just the two of us and would say, "Now look I've never heard of Dadaism so could you tell me?" I was so impressed that this is what a real scholar is all about, you are always asking questions, you are always open, always curious, rather than the assumption of—I know it all and what is this rubbish?

KC It only takes one good teacher doesn't it? You can abide the rest, one good teacher, a rare thing.

LH Yes. The university course was excellent because it didn't have anything much to do with criticism but rather a thorough knowledge of the texts from the earliest Old English right up to 1880, and . . .

KC Practically modern.

LH Yes, well . . . you could do modern literature as an option, but the person who was teaching this was pretty bad so I did Modern European Drama and Theatre technique as my special subject which took me into the 20th Century. But it was areas you wouldn't normally have gone into, say like learning Old English, which in the first two years is a real drudge, and in the third year was just marvellous when you got to read *Beowulf*. Equally 18th Century literature—Dryden, Pope, Swift and Sterne—great. You need to be pushed into that and not spend all your time on critical theory but getting to know the building bricks. And after you've done this degree which grounds you, then you begin to start learning. It's essential to becoming literate.

KC So what was the first sort of writing or creative environment you found yourself working in? When did it begin?

LH Sure enough from puberty, mid-teens, I wrote very bad poetry influenced by a combination of Keats, Wordsworth and T. S. Eliot—you can guess what the results were like, and then . . .

KC Neapolitan!

LH A dire little number. And then I discovered Pound—that was marvellous. But in terms of getting to meet writers and being more than just a solitary adolescent poet, it was when I was in London. And it wasn't university for sure, because there was no such thing as creative writing, the industry you get now, and there were no writers coming and talking. It was in Soho and various people I got to know in Soho in the cafes. There was a coffee bar called Sam Widges in Berwick Street, where I met Roger Mitchell, a painter, a curious man. He would stand by the juke box holding a large sunflower reciting some poetry and I thought "what on earth was that?" He gave me this slip of paper with four lines on it by Tristan Tzara—I was just so bowled over. I really hadn't seen this sort of thing done before. The language was terrific—I wanted more. I started scrabbling around and managed to find a small number of poems by Tzara. There was also a poet called Neil Oram, who owned Sam Widges.

KC It was an exciting atmosphere then—when was this?

LH 1959, '60, '61. Then gradually after '61, I was expanding into meeting friends of friends of friends, people on the London scene, like Pete Brown, Libby Houston, Spike Hawkins, the French poets Michel Couturier and Claude Royet-Journoud.

KC Okay—so, this atmosphere in which you first started to write seriously brings itself into the earlier poems?

LH It isn't just the literary scene, it was a whole blend of things. It was also the painting and the politics of the time. Going to an art gallery, like the Whitechapel Gallery, and seeing big shows of Jackson Pollock, Robert Motherwell. I was also going to the London anarchist group meetings, and this was the old anarchists, as half of them were old men who'd hidden in the Vienna Woods during the 1920s. Also there was CND and the anti-Nazi movement against the revival of Nazi Fascism in Germany. All of this mixing together made me aware of all the other stories that co-existed with mine.

KC And in those early poems—and I think part of the curiosity in them is what you've just said of this open, multiple, mixed-up world which isn't pure. In the introduction to the *Collected Poems* you also talk about the unreliability of language, whatever care you take it always remains unreliable and can trick you.

LH Yes.

KC You think you have it, but you don't have it—it's unfixed. And, we've already touched on this and the references you've made to other writers and painters. I think the untrustworthiness of language is a tension in your writing, but also in the early poems there is a very assured tone, it's an accomplishment. Alongside the surefootedness there's an interest in displaced locations, unexplained relationships, and a painterly abstraction in some poems, and the off-kilter and incomplete narratives which you've already touched on—they are stories but they're incomplete, they are slightly off-centre. Given all that mixture . . .

LH It's a big mixture!

KC . . . how do you make is so readable? Unpractised readers will come to your work, I've taught it to young students, their response is always on the lines of this poetry is so open. Maybe it's not an answerable question.

LH It's rather a difficult question to answer. The introduction you refer to was only written a couple of years ago and I don't think I was so conscious of that at the earlier time.

KC But still the tactics you were employing even early on suggested a distrust of language.

LH Well yes . . . I think I say in that introduction, but the language is all we've got? I believe that and trust people to read the words under the words, to see the heaping up of fragments, to see what's really happening underneath it all. Is it that working with fragments in some way reflects how the mind works, as Kitaj pointed out? We can be lost in thought, lost in cities, and be fooled into thinking the point is to find ourselves. Well, what would we do if we found ourselves anyway? You never can have that neat package. In fact, early writers like Gide, Stendhal, Henry de Montherlant relish the contradictions and complexity of human nature. I think my natural sympathy was for that tack—I probably haven't answered your question . . .

KC Perhaps not but what you've said is more interesting. Readable?

LH All I can say is that I've always felt that I'm talking to somebody, maybe it was myself, but I was talking to somebody. I'm not a writer on the page. I would always test what I'd written by reading it aloud—if it sounded right—if the music, no matter however disjointed that music might be, if it is what my ears want . . . so go with it..

KC So there is always an element of drama ?

LH Yes

KC Because if it is a person, a voice talking to another, it's on the edge of drama, isn't it?

LH Yes. All the words on the page are only a notation. The fact is they are physically spoken. The writing I like has a sense of being beyond the page, being heard, being thought about, just as you would think about what somebody says to you face to face.

If you read something only on paper you may never have quite that same dialogue.

KC Often your work sounds like something that one person might conceivably be saying to another.

LH Yes, though I'm very well aware that quite a number of people I've known could make neither head nor tail of what I write, but it wasn't intentional.

KC In a poem like 'The Argentine'—yes? Despite all the techniques and features you've described and which make for rearrangement, if not derangement, it's a typically sustained piece. There's a setting, an unexplained narrative, but its real business seems other than all of that—it's a series of intense emotional situations underneath. It's a feature which is the core of much of the early poetry, the charged atmosphere. There's also the arrangement of the inner and outer landscapes, which seems characteristic of other poems too at the time—'The Doomed Fleet', 'The Blue Mosque'. What was going on?

LH I can't remember what triggered these things except I just love writing stories, and, I suppose the stories came from a whole bundle of sources that probably a lot of people my age would have. In the 'Doomed Fleet' for example there are memories of *Battleship Potemkin*, First World War battleships and whatever.

KC Yes and we could, mistakenly or not, talk of you in terms of post-war poetry or as a post-colonial poet? There is a book called *The Sinking Colony*. It's a bit of a clue, isn't it? As a young man were you aware of the changing status of the UK in the world?

LH Certainly while I was at school I was really passionately against the Suez invasion in 1956. The year I was going to do my national service I just thought, why should I kill people or die for something useless like keeping Cyprus, or Egypt or Malaya.

KC The empire on its last legs.

LH In *The Sinking Colony* I think many of the sources are stories, inherited stories. There's an element of parable too but there are also actual incidents, personal and historical incidents. The speaker is there amongst all the other people in the story, with a particular passion or worry of that moment in that setting, even though it may not be happening in that setting.

KC Interestingly in 'Plato was right though' you seem to contradict some of that you've just described and you say that all the previous locations are now impossible. There seems to be a stripping off of what you've described as not exactly parables, the story-telling element. There's a contrast between this poem and others of the same time.

LH That poem is a bit didactic, especially the end which is unlike a lot of my work written at that time and after that time, but it was one of those moments when it all felt so useless. Yes, it was a stepping back. It starts off like a lot of those other long poems with a sort of toy landscape, like one of those pop-up alphabet books where you have a series of scenes. It goes into that imaginary world but then it shifts, and steps back and it's almost as though it's just going to talk about what really matters. Then the realisation the word 'love' does not suggest a strength or grace only ineffectuality and that language is so inadequate. In that way Plato was right to banish the poets from the republic because they were just so inadequate. It's a snipe at all the self-declared, bombastic poets who were talking as if their poems were going to change the world—in fact they are not going to change anything if they're coming out with that sort of facile stuff. The poem expresses a reservation.

KC I think that some of these elements we've touched on now, the difference between the typical poem like 'The Argentine' and the unusual poem like 'Plato was right though', show the way to 'The Sinking Colony'. In a very different way a similar moment occurs at the end of *The Man With Blue Eyes* in the poem 'Landscape with 3 people'. At the end of the poem there's the image of the ricks being burnt. Something valuable is lost, an innocence perhaps? It reads like the prelapsarian moment of the English pastoral coming to an end.

LH It is also that when I was a kid gangs of us would play in the hayricks and end up by almost wrecking them.

KC I think it has more resonance than that.

LH Yes, well, when you look at it. I suppose.

> 'I loved him and I loved her
> and no understanding was offered
> to the first citizen
> when the ricks were burnt.'

It's not a direct personal image, as we said earlier, the *I* can be the narrator. The *I* isn't necessarily me, it's the voice of the story. In fact the piece, the whole world of it, starts with ranches in South America, riding horses and so on, and then shifts to several different places. The third section is maybe London, as with the fourth, but what's happening at the end is—who is going to be blamed for burning the ricks? It's as though the narrator is to be blamed for the situation no matter what happens. There are other moments in the third section, about a simpler life, maybe with people who are not to blame, people in an ordinary working life with the sun setting who "lean forward to switch on television sets." There is that peaceful world without all this conflict. In a much later poem 'The Fern Cabinet', I quote, I think, Melville, on how whales protect their young when a ship approaches. The adult whales make a big circle and swim around to protect the young, who would be in the middle, and apparently the sea in the middle is immensely calm.

KC Innocence is under threat, is coming to an end there? The water is calm only because it is protected.

LH Yes, and it's always vulnerable to threat, threat from all sorts of forces, and it's a very fragile bubble. And it's partly that thing of blame. You can be blamed for burning the ricks though you didn't do it. Equally the person who is in love with a man and a woman can be blamed whatever happens—even though he meant well. So, as you say, a wider issue, or at least that's my view at this distance. There's a continual doubting in the poem, like the scene in the bookshop, 'most of this is far from true.'

KC But blame stays the same?

LH Yes. One of my experiences as a child—for whatever reason I was nervous—I was blamed for a lot of stuff that I never did. When I was accused of something I blushed and that confirmed I did it. I never did. So, yes, there's something personal there—but the poem's not about me, but somebody in that story is going to get blamed, and it'll probably be wrong.

KC A good deal comes together in those lines?

LH Yes, you don't know the full story, just part of it. I got a charge from writing it, but it's an extra bonus to feel that people reading it might get drawn into it, and they'll have to work out what happened outside of it, what happened next. Meanwhile, back at the ranch . . . The idea that the last line of the poem is there but in fact you hope it will keep rolling.

KC It has the virtue of incompleteness, which I've heard you speak about before.

LH Yes. This is true of anything, well not anything, but a lot of things I get pleasure from. When a book or a film finishes, I keep on with it. What can you do? This last winter I watched a *Midsomer Murders* episode; it's really bad TV, and I spent all night saying but that's impossible because so and so wasn't there, or whatever, and of course I had to work it all out and I couldn't. Well, I'm not alone in this.

KC Of course, it's why we admire detective writers. Now, coming to the end of this interview, and you've borne it bravely, this pursuit of the details and atmospheres of work from 40 or more years ago. Do you think you're the same person who wrote those poems? Do you look at them as though they were written by somebody else? You've denied being the rick burner, do you now deny being the person who wrote these poems?

LH I'm not the same person now as I was then. How could I be? It would be scary. A monster stuck inside a time-warp. But equally I know they're by me because my name is on the book.

KC Yes, you're to blame.

LH Yes, but when I look at these pieces I can remember all sorts of stuff, the fuller story, not just the things in there and so I know it's part of my history, something I made, but the person who made them is luckily no longer at this table.

KC Yes. I said earlier Lee, reading them again now, afresh, they don't strike me as an obvious type of young man's poetry and you said you'd worked all that nonsense off before hand. A typical note to me, what's that lovely phrase from 'Summer', that phrase, "the first hours/of confused ecstasies," well there's an atmosphere—suspended.

LH It seems . . . ah, well, accurate for a lot of people's experiences.

Sam Widges Coffee Bar, Soho, 1964.

The revisitation

Despite the dazzle of the New
—its own great and unique beauty—
(her long black hair reflecting a summer morning)
when the past's too roughly torn away
you can't deny the deep pain that
runs the length of my body
like the crack from an earthquake
that splits the new tarmac road
right down the middle for half a mile
Plate 56 in your geography text book
Its ragged lips have already tasted death
many times
An equatorial republic asking for aid
a large ship at anchor in the sound
a new pipe-line and harbour installations
the black capstan

(As a footnote—the escape was made
through a slim steel pipe which even you must know)
and that's enough said for now

Yet with this there is certainly no reason
for bitterness or resentment—they have no part
in this.
In fact there is nothing but the endurance,
there's not even a neat conclusion or clichéd saying
to draw on for cheap comfort—
only time and the inevitable process of a darkening
memory.
No one can be truly put at ease by this
as such inconclusiveness is always discomforting

The poem can always retreat
into an elaboration of the tropical scene
mentioned before, and time is passing
for all of us—isn't it?

Which island was it that the schooner
visited that year . . .

Dazzle

the dazzle of the New
—its own great and unique beauty—
(her long black hair reflecting a summer morning)
like the fresh white liner at anchor
in the sparkling blue sound of this Pacific island

An equatorial republic asking for foreign aid—
the large ship at anchor; a new pipe-line
and harbour installations; the glossy black capstan
and tar melting on the roads.
So many excuses and subsequent apologies
for the numerous blunders and inefficiencies
of my native workers—
the covers and symbols of my own astonishment
and love for you

But still I can't stop this wonder
that dumbfounds me every time I see you,
or, when alone, ever come to a full realisation
of what's happened and is still happening
and will continue happening.

I just gape at you
and know how I must appear so crazy
all red faced and sweating in the ridiculous
general's uniform of my small republic.
I am weighed down with gold braid,
epaulettes, medals, swords and nonsense,
as you pass in a light summer dress.

INTERVIEW 2 — NOVEMBER 2007

A defeating pink

KC Last time, we touched upon the world on which you first began writing. Can you tell me about the circumstances of the Fulcrum publication of *The White Room*, 1968 and *Landscapes*, 1969, I think?

LH And *The Sinking Colony* soon after that.

KC Did you have a view of your poetic career and was it influenced by the Fulcrum publications?

LH I don't think I had any awareness of career at that point, I wrote as a passion . . . I think Fulcrum was terrific because it gave me a far larger audience that I would ever have had with little press books. I was very lucky in the sense that I was in the right place at the right time. Before then you had duplicated, small press books which got around to very small numbers of readers, or you had the establishment people like Faber who were very, very conservative.

KC There was none of the access of print-on-demand.

LH No, then came Stuart Montgomery and Fulcrum and he changed it all. Just look at the list of books they published. Before that I just had two very slim books out. He wanted to publish a 120 page book of mine, hard covers, an edition of 3,000, and because he was so focused, not only did he do that, he made sure the books were reviewed, distributed. Very professional. He fixed tours to the States for me, something I'd never known before. The amazing thing was that with Faber—which had this snobbish attitude that it alone was real publishing—their editions of new writers were rarely more than 500 copies. Stuart was printing 3,000 and moving them.

KC So there are some reputations which were much bigger than their sales.

LH Yes, Faber really was kept afloat by its backlist. I wasn't conscious of careers. Maybe it's more prominent now with creative writing courses and so on. I think it was immensely encouraging just to have this publisher doing book after book of mine and staying there.

KC Yes but did it change the way you viewed it, Lee?

LH I'm not sure how, but you were in such great company. His list was so fine—Basil Bunting, David Jones, Roy Fisher, Lorine Niedecker, Gary Snyder, Ed Dorn and Robert Duncan, to name a few.

KC From the banda machine to international profile. Okay I've heard you read quite a few times and I want to ask you about readings. How do you prepare for a reading? Do you prepare, what do you do? You know it's a reading in a week's time, what do you do?

LH I'm very careful preparing for a reading. I find out how long they want me to read for. I then work out how I can fit the poems I want to read into the time slot. I have timings already for them or I will time them. I've got the whole reading mapped out beforehand and it's not only just to do with time but that within a programme there's a flow and a variety so that it doesn't get monotonous, so it's interesting and keeps the attention of the listener. So it's quite carefully worked out, it's professional and what one should do. Occasionally I will adjust a programme during a reading if I sense certain poems will work better with that audience. There are various people I know who will shamble on stage, flick through their books and say *I don't know what I'm going to read* and sort of read things at random. It maybe works sometimes, but other times it doesn't. It's the wrong emphasis, it's concentrating more on the personality of the poet and him doing this, or her doing this number, as opposed to someone coming on as a mouthpiece for the poems.

KC Right, so formal preparation?

LH Yes.

KC You don't talk much about the poems do you, when you read— it tends to be a little context but most of the time you spend actually reading the poem?

LH Yes—that's the intention.

KC Some poets talk an awful lot around them, don't they?

LH Basically, I've heard a number of poets over the years who talk endlessly explaining how the poem is written and what it's about and . . .

KC Which is always just so fascinating, isn't it?

LH Seamus Heaney would charm the pants off people and talk for about 10 minutes about this poem and then the poem lasts barely a minute.

KC That could be a blessing.

LH If you start telling the listener what a poem's about you're narrowing it. I don't explain too much, except maybe a few necessary odds and ends.

KC In terms of what actually happens when you read, or when anybody else reads, what do you make of that experience? You're standing there and actually reading the poetry—I always find the passing of time is an odd experience when you read to an audience. What's your experience of just actually doing the reading—what do you think, or feel when you do that? Does it all just go by?

LH No. All I know is that you can tell if a reading is going well, or not—so you are very conscious of that, whether you're on your toes or not. It's all to do with pace, and if you get your pace right and your tone right, it works and the people who are hearing are getting it. Whereas if you stumble, not getting it right, it just becomes an embarrassment—you think "What am I doing here?" But for me, the essential thing is that I'm talking to somebody. I may be imagining somebody in front of me I'm talking to as I'm reading the poem, even the person that poem might have been addressed to, maybe just talking to myself, but that somebody is my projection and it's also each member of the audience. I know this sounds a bit too grand, but . . .

KC No.

LH . . . but in one sense it must be in the manner of "talk" and overheard voices and so on.

KC So, when you read you don't feel like you are isolated off in a bubble—you're aware of a loop, of the audience response?

LH Yes.

KC Which can often be quite minimal, but it goes into the reading and then helps you to read the next one.

LH In a sense if you lose your contact with the audience, for whatever reason, then it just goes into the ground. And when I think of the writers I've really liked hearing read, such as Beckett's monologues and novels, it's a voice talking to you in your room, telling you this story. Or someone like Alistair Cooke, his *Letter From America*. There was a real warm, personal contact there.

KC Do you enjoy hearing others read?

LH If they read well. Recently there was a reading in London by Christopher Middleton and Marius Kociejowski, and Marius—I don't know what happened, but he read these poems which were stories and you were completely taken into this fascinating world. It is such a wonderful thing to experience. It was great. You also find this in the poems of Miłosz and Zbigniew Herbert, I so admire that. I so wish I could tell whole stories. My stories always get interrupted. Ah well. The other aspects of reading, beside talking person to person, is it's theatre.

It's not like a theatrical presentation, which does happen sometimes with certain people, but you have to think of all the qualities that an actor uses when presenting a part on stage, because in effect as a poet you are acting out the plot. You're reading out these words which in fact are not just your words.

KC It's been several decades you've been reading? I just wondered from your point of view whether the business of reading had changed very much over time. If you have any particular readings which seem to be of that time and typify certain atmospheres.

LH Readings have continued pretty steadily since the 60s and they're always going on. Sometimes you're Mr or Miss Popular and other times it's difficult, but the business goes on. As far as my own experience of reading, I didn't read my early work so well, but gradually over the years one gets more polished. I think I was very lucky in the 60s as there were a lot of recordings available and people visiting here who were really fine readers. I'm thinking of the LPs of Kenneth Patchen or Jack Spicer or Ezra Pound reading *The Cantos*. And Allen Ginsberg and William Burroughs coming over here and giving readings.

KC You were telling me the other day about a reading you did where there was a certain type of poet in the first half and a different type of poet in the second half. What was that about?

LH It was a poetry conference in Oxford and the first half was Roy Fuller, Elizabeth Jennings and Alan Brownjohn.

KC The heart does not beat faster.

LH They were the official poets. And then in the second half they had myself, Roger McGough and Adrian Mitchell. The audience in the first half were very respectful and silent because these were people of repute and in the second half they were relaxed and they thought, well this isn't poetry, but it is fun and they were laughing, they were reacting. It was a big theatre full of people and when I read I divided them up into different animals for my 'Central Park Zoo' poem and they loved it and liked all the stuff we gave them—moving around the stage instead of just standing at the lectern. Towards the end of our half this man got up from the front row, Sir John Waller I think, and he addressed the stage, "I think you young poets are really, really good but I have to leave", and he opened the door, which seemed to lead out of the theatre. As it closed behind him there were crashing noises, and then he staggered out the same door again. He'd gone into the broom cupboard. I think he needed a drink.

KC So he upstaged all of you really?

LH Yes, truly.

KC So readings have always been a part of what you do?

LH Yes because it's putting the poem out there. The poem on the page is, in one way, just a script. A reading makes it solid and real.

KC Okay, can we pick up now from the last interview and look at a few of the poems in detail? I had in mind the six poems of 'The Coast' at the end of *Landscapes*. I've read them and re-read them and they appear to mark a change.

LH This is a slightly roundabout way of answering your question but I've said that over the years I've been very lucky to have known three poets who very gently nudged me in the right direction— John Ashbery, Tzara and F.T. Prince. In 1967 I sent Prince the proofs of *The White Room*, and he wrote a nice encouraging letter—"but", he said, "you leave me with something of the same effect of garrulity—of having found a way to patter on."—and I thought *yes, you're right*. It was as though I had been too involved, when writing the book, with aspects of New York poetry, where you could produce yards of material. It was very lovely, but it was like, how many yards would you like? You become so practiced with a certain tone of voice. It really is a tone of voice. I could have gone on writing these poems forever and pleasing people. I thought, no this isn't why I'm here. I felt it was just becoming a clever tap-dance. I wanted something more real, no "real" isn't the right word, but I was becoming very dissatisfied with that earlier work and that voice. It needed somebody like Prince to come along and check me. It was already simmering but he gave me the license. This section of poems in 'The Coast', though they may be fragmented, are very immediate, bare, and tangible. It was a deliberate shift.

KC There's an objectivity with them, isn't there?

LH There was something said about Creeley once which ties this up. Creeley's ". . . rejection of the poetry of description and reflective arrangement in favour of the immediacy of the poem as event." That is akin to what I was trying to do.

KC Yes, which was my next question, about the broken lines and using that fairly prominent device of space for punctuation. I think another change is a more direct plaintive tone on the part of the person speaking the poem, that's noticeable, and what you've also touched on is a move towards literalism rather than the fiction.

LH Yes, that's from Prince's meticulous comments on words in my poems—it's like being more careful.

KC There's a distance isn't there between F.T. Prince and some New York poets?

LH Yes, but the weird thing is that he was very much admired by them. I first found out about Prince in New York. No-one knew about him here—well, very few people. Ashbery had included him in his *Art and Literature* magazine and then Ted Berrigan wrote a rave review of his *Doors of Stone* in *Kulchur* magazine.

KC Yes. So, there is a background story, there is a history to that stylistic and aesthetic change represented by 'The Coast'? Taking one of those poems, 'This Year': it's very tender, almost domestic but with something typical of you—there's a sensuality and an assurance, at ease with itself. Does that strike a chord, do you remember that poem that way?

LH I think these poems were trying to get a sense of immediacy, rather than be back in the past or in the future, and so they had a very physical and sensuous focus.

KC There are fewer words.

LH Yes. I was caught up with the idea of poems being part of an important telegram and the reader is only getting about half of the message and having to complete it. I like that principle, and again it's talking to the reader.

KC Yes—as an invitation to the reader.

LH The poet Joe Ceravalo published a book called *Fits of Dawn* in the mid 1960s. He used that punctuation with lots of spaces and I was really impressed by that, I thought that really works. Then later on, looking at Creeley's poems—he uses two or three words to each line. Again you're looking at these words as happening at this moment—being very physical.

KC As you say, it's a noticeable change.

LH Larry Eigner as well, who was published by Fulcrum, had a similar immediacy and similar layout.

KC Yes, so it's there in the air, it's happening with you and other people as well?

LH Yes.

KC Another one of those poems, 'Soft White', employs an almost hypnotic repetition. Do you think the phrase "meeting at a set of erotic points" could be a signpost here?

LH Yes.

KC And an almost geographical sensuality?

LH I'm not sure about geographical but certainly there's a sensuality to them. It's almost logging events as they're happening and so everything in it is tangible and you hope the reader as you mention something also thinks of that, touches their own hand.

KC The one that really strikes me, 'The Cliff Walk'—you are aware of the surroundings but there's a mystery about it as well. Did you write them as a run?

LH Yes they are pretty well in the order that they were written. That last poem, 'The Cliff Walk', it's shifting away. While I loved the idea of immediacy, I also felt it was too limiting, just as the idea of pattering on elegantly is too limiting. There are suggestions of stories, suggestions of past and present coming in, so it's a movement back, but in a modified way, to the stories of earlier work.

KC The person in the poem is merging into the world—there seems very little distinction between them—the person talking and walking around and the world in which he or she finds him or herself. The distance between the human and the natural is minimised isn't it?

LH Yes.

KC And I was going to say this clever thing about the green paint on the railing, the barrier—green being the imitation of nature. It's still wet and fresh, and it messes up the speaker's coat as he leans on the railing. Now you couldn't have been aware of that, you're not one of these clever, clever chaps who would have arranged such a complex symbolism, are you?

LH Well the green paint is, I guess, a symbol. Despite a wonderful view of the sea there's the danger of things going wrong, and once it's happened you're not going to get the paint off, you know. It's simple.

KC In the previous interview we spoke about how "I" is not always "you" in the poems—it's not always the person who it may appear to be, but sometimes is another. It seems to me that double poem 'Dazzle' and 'The Revisitation', and they are two separate poems but I think of them as a double poem, where you've reworked and played with that idea quite a bit. Can we talk about those two poems? What's the setting of 'Dazzle'— what's the framework of that poem, is there a framework?

LH I wrote them both on the same day, 5th June 1967, and they start with the same three lines. I wrote 'The Revisitation' first and then I looked at it and I just thought this poem could go in a very different direction, after the first three lines. So I wrote the second poem and, instead of dumping the first for the second revision, I thought they can coexist. They are like two sides of a coin, various things are mentioned in both of them but in different settings, though, some of the settings are the same. 'The Revisitation' is a very bleak poem and 'Dazzle' is like "Come on, it's not that bad." It's much perkier, warmer—it's a very full love poem. But 'The Revisitation' is as though things have a veil over them.

KC In stanza three in 'Dazzle'—there's quite a shift in the artifice about who's speaking this poem.

44

LH No. I just see it as being the narrator talking about how he's just in awe and amazed about this person he loves . . . so.

KC Well, come on, that's not a persona.

LH Ah! Well, no, I didn't say it was always a persona. Now and then it really is *me*, but I'm just one of the people in those scenes. In some of the poems I'm more centre-stage, in others I'm just beside the stage.

KC That's what I was trying to prompt you to say—that the persona can also be the autobiographical Lee, can also be the autobiographical *me*—that's part of the trick.

LH . . . yes . . .

KC That's what I thought—thank you.

LH The KGB had nothing on you.

KC My training's not gone to waste.

LH No, it hasn't—they recruited you at Cambridge didn't they?

KC That's a secret. I can't talk about it. 'Dazzle' is shorter—I don't know if sharper, certainly more emotional but disentangled.

LH Yes, the other one has more fictions and stepping outside the fictions and half way through the poem there's a footnote, looking at the actual writing of the poem.

KC 'The Revisitation' turns itself inside out a few times, loops the loop, whereas 'Dazzle' moves on. The speaker in 'Dazzle', this chap, with his "ridiculous / general's uniform", with all his medals and suchlike, what's he the General of, do you think, displacement, confused passion?

LH If you read the text it's of "my small republic . . ."

KC Oh right. Tell me where that is then?

LH Here. It's the narrator suddenly realising how all his fumbling around is a form of rhetoric. He's so foolish compared with the person, the loved one, who just passes in a light summer dress—she doesn't need all this clutter. The sweating General is a character that appears quite a lot, "One of life's corporals" in 'Take A Card Any Card' or earlier he's the person who burnt the ricks.

KC So does the small republic somehow transform itself into *The Sinking Colony*, Lee, is there a connection there as well?

LH It's in the air. I think it started with poems like 'Summer'—this trail of references to a particular time in history.

KC A post-colonial time?

LH Yes, when I grew up there was a whole body of stories that were shared. It was in the literature and novels of the time, the war histories, the memoirs. All those World War II films with submarines. There's all this stuff at the end of the empire and everybody knew it. It was quite a powerful series of myths. It's inevitable that it should be used as one of the materials in my work.

KC Yes, and the title *The Sinking Colony* is suggestive of that post-imperial phase?

LH Yes, it is. The Commonwealth disappearing and people, other than the exploiters, who had just tried to do a decent job, whether it had been installing railways or water systems, or whatever. They were all disappearing under the waves too as the colony sank, and there's the new society that took over, where they were irrelevant.

KC I think that's the emergent setting of the work from this time, it links with the characteristic sense of displacement as well. I don't mean a nostalgic longing for a better world when good chaps were in control, it's exactly not that. It's accepting displacement because you're not the centre of the world any longer.

LH Yes.

KC You're not the aggressor, the boss man—and the poems are off-centre as well, and kinder for it.

LH Yes—you are totally right. It's certainly isn't a nostalgia for that world.

KC So if we think about the *The Sinking Colony* there's a change in your writing at that point, all of these concerns coming together in it?

LH Yes. Over the years my work has swung between the puritan and cavalier routines but at each switch it has modified. So the poems in *The Sinking Colony* are often far sharper, more focused and particular and in a way serious, not playing around so much, but equally they're not bare.

KC They do incorporate a sort of fiction don't they?

LH Yes, a collage of a number of fictions.

KC They don't surrender everything to the fiction.

LH You're not sure what's fiction and what's real. Quotation marks are not to be trusted.

KC That's part of what I mean. Reading the piece makes you uncertain of the ground. You're not quite sure who's saying it, or has the poet made this up? Or is it a quotation from a real source that might turn the key?

LH This ties in with what we said earlier about producing works that demanded that the reader did a bit of work.

KC Yes, to characterise *The Sinking Colony* for someone who hasn't read it, I would say that there's a colonial setting and an assured speaker who is perhaps a colonial officer who finds himself in remote landscapes, sometimes troubled by quite hostile meetings. After the blending, the closeness and the sensuality of the poems of 'The Coast', the tone here seems to be about distance and departure rather than meeting? If we look in detail at something like 'Animal Days'—one of the devices is omission. What's going on there?

LH I think that omission is happening before in 'The Coast'. It seems the most accurate way of notating the way one's head jumps about, because things don't always come out in clear, rational arguments. 'Animal Days' doesn't work as a rational argument. It's a series of six different pieces, all collaged together, and I don't know quite how it works, but I trust it does. They're all coming in from different angles.

KC There are unresolved mysteries. Can the mystery at the beginning of the poem be named, should it be, or is it best left unnamed?

LH There's a wonderful Elizabeth Bishop quotation. What she loves in poetry is ". . . accuracy, spontaneity, mystery . . ." I've only read that recently but I realised it was so appropriate to what I loved when I was writing those pieces.

KC It's an odd combination of three qualities, isn't it?

LH Yes. Taking 'Animal Days' I did a breakdown of what's happening. In the first section you start off with a two line quote from Lieutenant Colonel Wintle, from the book he wrote *The Last Englishman: The Autobiography of Lieutenant Colonel A. D. Wintle, MC*. He was one of the last British cavalry officers. In some ways you would think an unattractive person, but, in fact, he was a marvellous person. His sister was swindled by a Brighton lawyer who had the courts and everything stitched up. Wintle just sold all his personal property and pursued this man relentlessly until years later in the House of Lords he won his case. The Lords said they'd never heard a case like that argued so well, and he conquered the clever lawyers by just sheer honesty. He just felt his sister had been wronged, just as again, at the start of the Second World War, there was a very incompetent Air Marshall who was a politician—he wasn't really an Air Marshall—who just screwed up everything and Wintle went into his office and pulled a revolver on him to just make him wake up. He was costing people their lives. Wintle was put in the Tower for treason and then he demanded "Well, charge me, I want a court martial", and they wouldn't—they knew what would come out. And so, okay, you think of the last British cavalry officer and he's a figure of fun, but in fact you see, no, don't be fooled by these caricatures. There are people there, like Wintle, who are really honest, decent men. And so there are his two lines, "The polo season would start in early April, so there's no time to be wasted." It's—so let's get on with it. So straightforward. You start with a Wintle quote and then there are fairy stories, and then paintings like Crivelli's *The Annunciation* come in.

The second section starts with my father at Dunkirk. He was a meticulous man, a maths teacher. The soldiers were throwing a lot of equipment and rifles away and he insisted all his men kept their rifles. He cared for them very much and got them off in one piece, a bit like Wintle. Then comes working in Great Witcombe as a forester, a personal account of that. The third section starts with some maxims and then you get Red Indians, then you get the forest, then a 19th century explorer's book, which is a fake quotation I made up. In the fourth section, you get a medieval renaissance painting, then the forest. The fifth section of the poem is working in Great Witcombe then a medieval setting again, a colonial quotation I think that's made up, and ends with a rhythm and blues song lyric. And the sixth, it's personal at the beginning, then It's about the forest and the jungle and a mission station and ends up with this castle. Now how would you put all that stuff in a bag? But somehow it works. In that poem. It's how one is beset by violence and cruelty, and how one misses opportunities to get things right, or screws up because of just not saying the right thing in the right time. But somehow it's simple. Your survival will be possible because of your tenderness and doing your duty. It's about besieged decency from all sorts of different angles and using different myths and sources, but it does work.

KC That's a very telling phrase—besieged decency.

LH Well, in section five of the poem there's an account of picking a rabbit up. I was working as a farmhand, harvesting a grain crop. The rabbits were being driven into this shrinking central area as the combine went round and round in ever decreasing circles. The dogs would be circling around waiting for the rabbits to make a run for the edge of the field. I came across a really small rabbit who was crouched down in terror and I just picked it up and held it to me, walked to the edge of the field and released it into the brambles. The feel of the rabbit against my chest—its heart beating—that tenderness—we're all in this together.

KC We're all encircled. So there is a common feeling despite the decentred and detached nature of the six parts. Something joins them.

LH Yes, there are various strands weaving their way through this tapestry.

KC To call the poem in a sense decentred is not right actually?

LH At a first reading it might be seen as that, but in fact if you read it carefully and then go back and forth you realise there are constants.

KC We have to puzzle the connections through. If we look at the poem 'The Sinking Colony' as well, did you want part of it to sound like a colonial servant's diary or a sort of log book?

LH It works in a very similar way to 'Animal Days', except each of the six sections is more continuous. They are less fragmented, fewer jumps. It's a mixture of prose and poetry. The first section is like a spoof memoir—I don't think spoof is the word—of a geologist working for the colonial service in India in the late 19th Century. And, then there's another section like 'Canadian Days' with lumberjacks working in the forest in Canada. There are a couple of stories like that. It's a collage that I hope accumulatively grows into a whole and it soaks into the reader rather than is explicit. It's strange and it's also tied up with the André Gide quote at the beginning, that you can't always judge things by their appearance. The Gide quotation is "This might almost make one suppose that he loved Bernard? . . . No; I think not. But a little vanity is quite as effectual in making us pose as a great deal of love." There's a similar thing in *The Long Black Veil* where there is a quote from Stendhal. This man and woman are passionately in love, but in fact they are more in love with the idea of their affair than they are as people. There is this surface layer in the poem but what's going on underneath that story?

KC If we look at the end of the poem, part six, the tone is quite ambiguous, the emotions mixed, the people stumble in, they sound like they've been chased or in danger. What's going on?

LH Part six pulls together a lot of the threads of the earlier five sections. The people stumbling into the clearing could well be protagonists who caused trouble in the previous section. A fight was starting even though it wasn't intended. Everything is falling down again—a house of cards in a way—all the fictions are collapsing and, despite all of this, it is wrapped up by the last lines, "even in the dreams we all needed one another . . .". The fictions are slightly dream-like. There are also parts in the poem

51

which double-check the actual poem. Section four has three lines printed in italics which are a spoof nature poem, as though we are going to continue in this manner. Then "Haven't we been here before? / (sigh)"; It's a lot of rugs being pulled from under people's feet and from under the poem's feet.

KC That happens towards the end but we have a series of illusions and deliberate wrong tracks. There's confusion and mysteriousness. At the same time the unifying emotion, that even in dreams we all needed one another. So it's not just displacement is it?

LH No.

KC There's something wrapped up in this mystery, it doesn't just disperse?

LH No it doesn't. It's not just an exercise in technique.

Lee Harwood on Palace Pier, Brighton, 1971.

Charles de Gaulle Airport—Roissy

for Jud

cool gliding corridors of steel and glass
hung in the air — that amazing
display of elegance "city of the future"?

(So this is what Futurism means??
and this my first Futurist poem??)

and yet amongst all this "comfort"
I only think of you,
of a plain wood table in the kitchen
sitting drinking coffee together
the small garden outside
the cats demanding as ever

I "wax pastoral" as they say
in my love for you and the life we make
but know what this means
and its value

Now here surrounded by these elegant machines
and graceful forms — buildings that
yes, men have built
I cannot say
what but that in no way
rejecting them I have to live
by the simplicities I know

Swimming the Atlantic

KC From 1970 to 1981 you wrote three very different books and I wondered if we could talk about the differences, connections and similarities between those three works *The Long Black Veil, Boston–Brighton* and *Wine Tales?*

LH In order to answer that I've really got to go back to what we talked about earlier which was these two strands, and how sometimes, well often, they interweave, but sometimes they're separate. There's the one which is writing that is simple, factual, direct which works in 'The Coast' and *Boston–Brighton*. And the other one which is baroque stories and quite a few trimmings, which is Cavalier as opposed to Puritan. *The Sinking Colony* is Cavalier, and *Boston–Brighton* is Puritan, to put it crudely. *Wine Tales* delights in stories, it's not obviously trying to have a direct tone to it, so Cavalier again. *The Long Black Veil* is a weave of both those strands.

KC *Wine Tales* is a collaboration with Ric Caddel. How did the two of you set about writing it? Is it your only collaboration?

LH No, I've done three or four other ones. Later on I did one with Tony Lopez called *Wish You Were Here*, one with Ian Robinson, though in the end Ian didn't write his half, called 'Five Pieces For Five Photos' and more recently I wrote 'Gifts Received' which is a set of six poems sparked by gifts received, whether it be a bus ticket or a fruit wrapper or a quote from somebody's dream. Also in the 1960s I wrote collaborative poems with Peter Schjeldahl, John Ashbery ('Train Poem') and a couple of others.

KC So those were different styles of collaboration?

LH Yes. *Wine Tales* is the one which is the most total collaboration as opposed to writing parallel texts sparked by the same material.

Ric and I had a lot in common, shared enthusiasms, including wine drinking. Ric was visiting me in Brighton and we were talking about the wonderful labels you used to get on wine bottles and the stories you could make up to go with them. I'd already done one from a Claret label. So we decided on a collaboration where one of us would choose a wine label, start a piece, send that to the other who would complete that piece. They would then choose a wine label, start a piece, send it back for the other to complete, and so it zigzagged back and forth between the two of us.

KC So that really is a very close, intimate collaboration, isn't it?

LH After we'd finished all this we went through it, and rearranged the order of the labels a bit, so it worked better as a book. We also edited it slightly so the joins weren't so obvious in several pieces. We don't say in the book who wrote what.

KC So there's no way of saying "I wrote that one, Ric wrote that one." It's a genuine collaboration isn't it?

LH Yes. The idea was sparked by a poem by Raymond Roussel called 'La Source'. It's a long poem in strict verse form. A narrator is sitting in a restaurant with a bottle of mineral water and there's a scene, a landscape, on the bottle. He walks into the landscape. It's a long description of what he sees. Right at the end, he comes out of the label, back to the table in time for the waiter to arrive with his lunch. I loved that idea. We were spoofing various tones of voice at the start, but things crept in we didn't expect to happen and we had to deal with them, which was great. For instance, if I'd ever tried to write about my father directly at that point, I couldn't. But for some reason, there are pieces there that are very much about my father.

KC It lifted the lid on it for you.

LH Yes.

KC And you weren't actually thinking perhaps about that subject at all.

LH Yes, it was just a story from the labels. Something outside us.

KC So as with the Roussel, it begins, you go into the label, the references and responses themselves expand and diversify into unexpected areas, as you have said yourself, but also the cast list is quite curious. Anthony Barnett and Sabu the Elephant Boy, for instance, don't seem to be immediate partners, but they are there in the writing. A typical Harwood phrase, "the enchanted calm" occurs as well. What's going on here?

LH I don't know. You start on something and the poem takes over and carries you along. In 'Claret', the one which has Anthony Barnett in, and Sabu the Elephant Boy, I was thinking about a train journey and all the worlds you pass. And then for some reason I associated the tone of a pompous statement with Anthony Barnett, who I hope will forgive me, but who is inclined at times to brag. Maybe he didn't say he was the greatest xylophone player in Norway, but he came very close. So it just popped in and in a collaboration you can indulge yourself because you can always edit it out later.

KC You think we're going to edit this out later, don't you? But we're not. Perhaps Anthony does possess such musicianship.

LH Sabu is childhood again. I remember as a child going to Brittany and going to the film show which was in the village hall, with the priest working the projector. There was a showing of Sabu The Elephant Boy and the projector would often break down and people would start talking, making gags, and the priest would rush out and threaten everybody and say "If you don't shut up I'm not going to show the rest of the film." And we'd all quieten down and then get a bit more of Sabu.

KC It is a playful sequence, in many respects, isn't it?

LH Yes.

KC Moving on then to *Boston–Brighton*. Is it a sequence, or a Jack Spicer serial poem, a logbook, or just a collection of poems? There's a plaintive lyricism and documentary style, the story telling and then that element which is striking, that bare vocabulary, the style of poems like 'Chen', for instance. And maybe we could look at some of those styles as exemplified in 'Sea Journals', 'Charles de Gaulle Airport–Roissy', and 'Portraits from my life'.

LH The original *Boston–Brighton* book was almost all very direct, simple and factual. Those three poems you mentioned at the end were written at the same time but weren't included in the original book because they didn't really fit. They were more baroque. When I came to assemble the *Collected* I realised I liked them, so I slotted them in that section. The *Boston–Brighton* book wasn't a conscious, Jack Spicer sequence. It was really a combination of a log book and a collection of poems written during that time I was in Boston and when I was first back in Brighton working for the Post Office. I realised as they accumulated, especially the Boston section, that it was a unit. There are personal accounts of living in Boston, but they are very factual. It's also about different maritime museums, the details of a street in Maine, Kennebunkport, and Boston historic sites. The short poems are set in a context, in a landscape. I wanted to get back to a bare, direct poetry which this is, especially the Boston section. This was after I'd returned from Greece where I'd started writing very simple pieces. Also this approach was in the air. A lot of people were still very keen on Charles Olson's *Maximus* and William Carlos Williams's *Paterson*. In Britain a lot of poets, for better or worse, were interested in bringing history and geography into their work. I eventually found out it was a dead end. It had become too formulaic. I know lots of poetry where people have done a lot of research but it really doesn't work as a poem.

KC As you say, it's in the air and it picks up in the poems.

LH There are also other aspects, too, in the respect for ordinary things. In that piece 'Kennebunkport' the influences aren't just American. There are elements of Surrealism. Novels like *Paris Peasant* by Louis Aragon, or Andre Breton's *Nadja*. In *Nadja* there's a passage where the narrator is waiting for somebody in a square in the suburbs of Paris. There's a statue of a very minor dignitary in the middle of the square, and all the objects in the square become mysterious. It's looking at the things you would normally take for granted, then seeing how strange they are.

KC That's one feature of the book. Another is in a poem like 'Charles de Gaulle'. I think it brings together typical features of your writing. It's clearly an occasional piece isn't it?

LH It was written straight off, pretty well. You land at this brand new airport, all this luxury and wealth about, and yet despite this I felt where I really wanted to be was sat back around the kitchen table with my wife Jud. Not that I'd want to criticise the wonderful architecture but I'd really liked to have been home. It's quite simple.

KC What I see is that the poem is stripped down as it progresses, it says more the simpler it becomes.

LH It's a territory where there really aren't any words—you can only have hints.

KC You play a similar trick with that poem 'Portraits from my life'— we think we're going to be told something about your life, and we're not are we?

LH Not directly, no.

KC What are we told?

LH It's very much about various paintings I love a lot and the echoes they stir in me and stories they suggest. What comes out is to do with essentials. By using this indirect way you can describe them more accurately, where an attempt to say those things directly would be clumsy if not impossible. You can tell a lot about people by what sort of books they read, or what sort of music or painting they like. It's just like the later 'Take A Card Any Card' which was sparked very much by all the pictures I have on my walls. Wherever I've been I've reassembled these various combinations and I wonder "Why do I do this, why do I keep them there?" The reason must be they really matter to me in some ways I'm not fully conscious of, and logging not only what it is in those pictures that matters but also the connections between them, it gives you quite an accurate map of my values, but in an indirect way.

KC Yes, the virtue of the indirect gaze, if you look directly at something and think you're going to write about it, it falls apart. If you think you're writing about a wine label, your father arrives. The alternative poetry is always the poetry of the personal or public crisis isn't it? It's not in short supply. Another really interestingly involved piece, *Sea Journals*, really struck me again when I read it this time around. Quite a long and extended piece, that follows its nose down different rivers?

LH You have very direct factual concerns, which are almost akin to the voice in 'Notes of a Post Office Clerk', but can't resist putting in stories as well. You have these two parallel worlds, one is actually on the coast and the other one is obviously the imaginary ship which is off the coast looking back at the coast. It's going back and forth and the combination of these maybe is a more accurate summary than to have one narrow story.

KC There's an openness to it and it seems that much of the experience is open to the poetry as well, that it's available to the poetry. It reads in an odd way, like a log book or a diary, doesn't it?

LH Yes, especially the stuff on the coast. Off the coast is like stories, but equally they could be the stories you might be daydreaming when on the coast, so they're real.

KC I think we've finished with those two books and I want to move onto *The Long Black Veil* now. *The Long Black Veil* is at the beginning of this time 1970–81, so I've deliberately gone backwards through these books. It's one of your best pieces, it's a marvellous poem. How did it come to be written? It's certainly a love poem but more than that.

LH The origins of it were a series of lyrics, like a long love poem, mapping the history of a relationship. I realise that far more happens than that. In terms of the actual writing of it I think I started in about 1970, writing these lyrics, not sure what was quite happening with them. A few of them were published in the first issue of *The Poetry Review* which Eric Mottram edited, in the autumn of 1971. The final version wasn't finished until July 1972 by which time, besides various corrections made to the lyrics, thanks to F.T. Prince, it was complete. At one point he criticised me, saying there was a phrase "I fuck you" and he'd said "you wouldn't really say it to anybody would you?" And, I thought, "no you wouldn't." I looked at the words more carefully. The thing was that the set of lyrics were too thin. They needed more of a tangible landscape and structure to give them solidity, to make them credible. What I did was an extension of what I'd done in earlier poems, where if you include in a scene, say two lovers in a room, the fact of a car back-firing in the street outside, it suddenly becomes much more real. It also becomes real for the reader because it's not claustrophobic.. The narrator of the poem is watching this scene, people in the room and outside there are others walking the street as the car back fires. So you're creating a world any reader can look at like a film.

KC So it transformed itself as it grew and became more than just a collection of lyrical pieces about that relationship?

LH Yes, the landscape which is described isn't just a side issue. You've also got the literary parallels and all sorts of other questions come up. The preface, for example, asks what do you do with memory, the power and the use of memory, and what is this power and why is it so powerful?

KC When poems accumulate you get further and further from the original experience.

LH Yes, that seems like an accurate account of how the human brain deals with the things you store in your head. I suppose it's talking about the power of memory and the danger of memory in the sense that it can become a concept and therefore actually distort what actually happened and take you away from the actual present into a false world.

KC It spins a cover over itself all the time?

LH Yes, memory after memory dug up again and again can become dangerous, a false rewriting of the past. But It can also be very valuable. It can be an essence of what really matters to you— that's why it stays in your head so long.

KC Robert Sheppard has an interesting phrase. He talks about your poetry being at once "distanced and intimate". That seems to be exemplified in this book, I would have thought, in terms of the different conversational elements you have in the poem. Some of these couldn't be more intimate and yet there's a reach beyond personal memory through to ancient archetypal figures and iconography.

LH It moves back and forth. It steps back and looks at the story, then it goes back into the story. You're double-checking saying is that real, and equally sometimes stepping back even further saying it's only writing anyway.

KC There's a range of sources and quotations throughout the sequence. One particularly striking element is that which you take from ancient Egyptian mythology. What prompted that feature, it's not just a clever piece of dressing up, is it—it's ingrained in the whole sequence. How did that get into this transatlantic poem about being in love—because Egypt isn't in the middle of the Atlantic is it?

LH Not the last I heard, no. The simple fact is that at one point in the relationship I was in Boston. The Museum of Fine Arts there has an amazing collection of Egyptian statues and I was especially struck by a statue of King Mycerinus and his wife, and also the same king with the goddess Hathor, and a local deity. There was a tenderness in these statues with the pharaoh's wife, or Hathor, reassuring, holding the pharaoh up. There was a lovely equality of men and women which I'd never really seen before. In so much European sculpture you very rarely get men and women together and certainly not as equals. I was very impressed by this, because it seemed to portray an essence of something I valued a lot.

KC When I read this again, what strikes me is that it is a poem about absolute love, about complete possession by love—*agape* is the Greek word.

LH Yes.

KC And at the same time you know you are not the only person in the world who's found this, now or in the past. Perhaps that's another reason for the Egyptian iconography?

LH Yes, that's true. There are lots of parallels in the work of other events which are like this love scene. Sometimes the parallels are critical of it and sometimes they are akin to it. You have in Book 3 a country setting, upstate New York, where you find this sort of courtliness, what would be called country manners, country and western manners. That sort of care and politeness is parallel to the actual love—it's a form of love. And then there are double-checks on this like the Nicholson quote. This is all in Book 3. A lot of things rattling around in there which are saying yes, this is a story, but it's one of many stories and with all the usual developments and changes you would expect from a story teller. Later on you have the quote, I think it's in Book 6, from Stendhal about "the intense love". In fact the love on that occasion was people not so much really loving each other but being in love with being in love, also feeling flattered that the other person should love them. It was a more selfish event. With all these little things which are akin to the main story, whether it be Stendhal or the Egyptians or the country manners, they're continually questioning the main story. There's much more to the story.

KC Yes, indeed, but at the same time the love lyric addressed to the beloved?

LH It's what it's about.

KC It's nothing without that, is it?

LH No.

KC I've heard you read the whole poem on one occasion and it's the passion that comes through. Rereading begins to explain the reason for all the other material which accompanies the passion. Books 1, 3, 7, 8, 9, 12 contain very direct lyrical statements. It's a remarkable quality. You've spoken about this but let's say some more about the relationship between the sustained emotional experience and all this other material. It's something I want to develop when we look at the 'Unfinished Opera'. The apparently diverse elements lend themselves to one another, they make each aspect clearer in the process. Does that make sense? This is intimacy and distance again, isn't it?

LH It is giving a more thorough picture. A love story is in reality far more complex and has far more contradictions in it, as we all know, than would be imagined generally. In Egyptian mythology the gods are immanent in nature, they are part of the world around you, just as the dead are. You stand there, the dead are all round you holding you up, supporting you. The past is that which is always around you. Later on in that poem 'African Violets' for my grandmother, it's as though "Right, she's gone but the values she left me with will be with me forever. She's still sitting in the chair saying 'That's a bit extreme isn't it?'"

KC She was probably right.

LH Yes. In Book 11 there's the phrase, "the ghost that guides us". *The Long Black Veil* is a parting.

KC It's a burial, isn't it? A preparation for a burial?

LH Yes, but in that history there's so much that goes on after that sustains one.

KC Again I'm struck by the Egyptian material. It's almost as if you've stumbled across an archetype, waiting in the museum, which is right there in the experience, in the blood. After thousands of years it's still there which makes it strangely impersonal at the very moment of absolutely personal experience.

LH I suppose what you were saying earlier about *agape*, the love— it's not been the only time a person has been in love, but a long tradition of this, and I'm not talking about the medieval courtly love tradition. It is far more basic than that.

KC So just describe those two statues again.

LH On one statue of the pharaoh, his wife is standing on his left, she has her right arm around his waist and her left arm goes across and she rests her hand on his left upper arm. And in the other statue . . .

KC They both look straight ahead, don't they?

LH Yes, and in the other statue Hathor is doing the same thing to the pharaoh. It is a wonderfully tender, I don't know whether reassuring is the word, gesture which seems so much to catch the tenderness of deep love, set in stone.

KC So you present the intimate, the close experience, and the distant, to use Robert's terms about intimacy and distance. There's a technique of sincerity here, which is more than the pouring out of your heart, isn't it?

LH The intensity which is seen in the poem by Ibn' Arabi which says "God's face is the face of your lover." That is real. That cannot be treated ironically, but equally you know that within the poem there would be a sentence that would remind us of all sorts of complexity in what seems a simple story. I'm probably repeating myself now but the quote from E.M. Forster praising Gide for registering that complexity, it's essential to writing. The two must be strapped together.

King Mycerinus and his wife.

Desert phone

My heart melts at the sound of your voice,
at the sight of your words.

Our long history on small scraps of paper.

We cross the river and then, in the willow grove beyond,
prepare for the next stage,
go straight on even, our clothes still dripping with water.

And later
as though lost on the plain,
scrub bushes, canyons, the hot flat desert
with rolling blonde hills on its edges
and the arid mountains beyond.

How did we get here? we ask ourselves,
too hot to cling to each other for safety
and instead, dazed, seem to wander in circles.

No wise words, only a vague hope and trust
that waves like a mirage, falters
with the light breeze at evening time.

I can talk of your nakedness or your fire
but I won't.

What is the thin green line on the horizon?
Tree tops that line a cool steep valley?
another river?

The beams in the house are rotting, need replacing.
Too much weight? The burning blue
sky pressing down.

Interview 4 — January 2008

Our long history on small scraps of paper

KC If we can start with *All The Wrong Notes* which was the first book of yours I read, so all the errors I make now are my own. I wonder if it was written in part as a movement away from the more organised books that come before it? Can you tell me how it was compiled—if that's the term? If there is a method, does it carry over to *Rope Boy to the Rescue*? So, how was *All The Wrong Notes* written, compiled?

LH It wasn't a reaction to the large structures like *The Long Black Veil* or even a book like *Boston–Brighton*. It was more a gathering of poems that arrived during a period, though by the time the book was ready to be published I had had time to pull out various ones that were weaker and shape it into a book. It wasn't a book as a conscious unit, but it was an assembly of poems that would always have common threads.

KC The original book published by Pig Press also included photographs?

LH Yes, photographs of street scenes in Brighton by Judith Walker/ Jud Walker.

KC Was *Rope Boy* put together in the same way? There's a much tighter framework there isn't there—it's written much more quickly.

LH I wouldn't say it's a tighter framework. I think it did assemble itself in the way that *All The Wrong Notes* did except I didn't have so long a period to mull it over and subsequently I feel *All The Wrong Notes* is a much tighter book. *Rope Boy* is a bit more of a ragbag of poems where some of them might have been dropped.

KC I wonder if we could look at poems in *All The Wrong Notes* which typify those different elements, which may or may not connect— something like 'You Essai: You OK' and 'A poem for writers'? Is the instruction to keep all the wrong notes in a declaration about that scope and openness of the work?

LH Yes, it is. The Charles Ives quote, his insistence that the wrong notes can be right, and even if some of these seem odd or sentimental, one should be able to include them because they're part of the whole. I think it's also about a question of trust, that the reader should trust, well to a degree, the writer. Ives's copyist thought they were the wrong notes, but in fact they were right. He should have trusted Ives to know what he was doing. And so equally within these assemblies, which may seem too disconnected, just stick with it and see how the whole works. It's as if the poems are a chemical reaction, all these different particles soaking into you, the reader. It's how it operates rather than it being a worked out sequence—a to b to c to d . . .

KC So some of those surprising interruptions, or what appear to be interruptions, are not always gentle? You'll go from a confirmative piece to the Holocaust which seems to shake the poem at the end.

LH There's a two part answer to that in the sense that I think shaking is essential in all the poetry that I enjoy. The problem for me in reading mainstream poetry is that it pleases people as it confirms their prejudices. I want to read things in a fresh way, to question things, or be sprung into a new area. As far as that reference to the Holocaust, well that is very particular. It's part of a pair of poems entitled, what was it?

KC 'Posters'.

LH Yes, 'Text for two posters by Ian Brown'. The two posters, which were commissioned by South East Arts years ago, argue with each other. The first one is questioning ideas of perfection and how life isn't like that. A face is not symmetrical, nothing in nature is symmetrical, and going on from that to underline the grief that the search for perfection can give us. The second poster, which again moves back and forth and argues with the first and parallels it, lists the need for having dreams, for having perfection, for seeking it whether it be love or whatever. But at the end having a reminder, a very sharp reminder of what can be the fruit of perfection in some circumstances, which in terms of European history and the idea of an Aryan nation and Hitler's dream of the perfect Germany that involved the slaughter of millions of people. So sometimes it's better to just shamble on with the imperfections, which is probably a more human way than having these big ideals.

KC Before the reference to the Holocaust, I think you write about where the wind might blow us and fearing the wind. Sometimes the wind can lead to odd places, can't it?

LH Yes, the line is 'how the wind blows and our hearts ache to follow the hazardous route the winds follow'. Before that are all sorts of scenes of beauty and perfection in nature and the wonders of history, of buildings, and everything around us.

KC We've jumped ahead, in fact, what I was going to ask you about was the poems 'You Essai: You OK' and 'A poem for writers' as examples of keeping the wrong notes in. This element of the gallimaufry which seems to be a sort of compositional concern in the book. You want an artful rag bag. Can we talk about one of those poems?

LH 'You Essai: You OK' is an address to my friend Paul Evans but the poem spreads far wider than that. A lot of it is echoing the posters. The forces of darkness, cruelty, are repressive to more open, generous and gentle forms of behaviour and decency. It's prefaced by a quote from Albert Camus, "Once again the

71

philosophy of darkness will dissolve above the dazzling sea." That also echoes those lines in *Return to Tipasa* by Camus, "On certain mornings, as we turn the corner, an exquisite dew fills our heart and then vanishes. But the freshness lingers, and this always, is what the heart needs." Someone walks around a corner, what they see just bowls them over. It's marvellous. But you also have various repressive things happen in section 2, *1900*, which is based in a real placed called Hotel Wolf in Wyoming. It ends up with a very grim scene, an atrocity, a cart pulled by gauchos having been filled with heads. It's factual. Section 4 talks about the barbarity in the Second World War and how Colonel Georges said he finally wrote an account of his experiences, not that he wanted to, but he was saddened by the fact that all the stories of the Resistance were becoming myths. Where's the reality, where are the facts? The actual history was far more important, the details of humanity rather than the grand claims. This comes up again in the last section, 5, to do with trade unions. You know, the cliché "In union is strength", but it's true. It's odd to meld these things, maybe for some readers, but they are true and one shouldn't be censored from including them.

KC You acknowledge that though don't you, by the description of the banner "I can't make out the motto", it's tucked away in a corner of the museum isn't it?

LH Yes.

KC If we look at a poem like 'A poem for writers' it seems to me that you engage the same technique but in a more concentrated form, that it's not in sections but almost from stanza to stanza.

LH That's accurate. It's like a series of steps, like a picture within a picture within a picture, almost.

KC It's as if you're discarding the artifice as you go. Also in 'Plato, Dante, Pound & Co give up but try'. What interests me, I think it's there in the whole book and in *Rope Boy*, is that you take the limits of the poetry into the making of the poem itself. Perhaps this relates to the ethics of inclusion in the book? There's submission at the end of 'A poem for writers', but also an ambition. In the second half of the title of 'Plato, Dante, Pound & Co give up but try' that's the state of mind.

LH You've got to at least try even though you may not be successful, probably won't be successful. It's realistic about the limits of language and communication and again this is something we talked about before. There are times when as near as you can get are hints or suggestions. It's going to the edge of the thing, and in a way giving yourself or the reader a push so they can somehow sense what this is, even though you may not be able to put it into words. In a strange way non-communication is communication.

KC You take that limitation and bring it into the poem as well.

LH Yes, that's what I was trying to say. In the first section of 'Plato, Dante' there's a line "let the wind speak, that is paradise", which is from Pound. I think that is saying the same thing—you can't describe paradise, you just lie listening to the sound of the wind—that's paradise.

KC There is something characteristic in the aesthetic of the book—a maturity? How old are you by now in this book?

LH I was out of short pants that's for sure. I was 40.

KC In this book and the books that follow, there's a stepping in and out of the artifice. For instance, the stories in *Dream Quilt* are varied in tone and topic, but the story telling is constant. There are stories for children, accounts of family history, colonial fables, stories about great scientists, stories by your children, scraps of a long history which is both personal and historical. You write as a son, a grandson, as a father, as a friend. There's so much you'll let us see about how this is made, and so much that is hidden.

LH But it's not a conscious hiding. The original intention of *Dream Quilt* was starting stories or presenting a couple of paragraphs from the middle of a story and wanting the reader to continue with it. The whole book is 30 such starting points. It's like the exercises I used to have as a child at school. You'd be told to write an essay starting "When I was on holiday . . ." or something like that. There's also the structure of the book. It's like a quilt where all the pieces work together as a whole and accumulatively give the reader, I wouldn't say message, a certain sort of approach, a sense of things.

KC You've spoken about it as if the 30 stories are extracts from 30 other works, continuing elsewhere. We just have the tip that shows—is that part of it?

LH Yes, I think, *Dream Quilt* is akin to 'You Essai: You OK'. Miłosz says "The purpose of poetry is to remind us how difficult it is to remain just one person. Our home is open, there are no keys in the doors, visible ghosts come in and out at will." So, yes, you can be consciously writing something but equally all sorts of things can come your way, which you follow and trust and the result is surprising and terrific, one hopes.

KC And *Dream Quilt* is one example, a house with 30 rooms?

LH Yes and there's some very odd people in there.

KC I want to pursue this idea, this stepping in and out of artifice. If we take a very different poem, 'Desert Phone', which begins "my heart melts at the sound of your voice, at the sight of your words", that's a very striking beginning.

LH I don't think so.

KC You're wrong.

LH I see it as a literal sequence of events.

KC But that's why it's striking—it's the very literal power of it that strikes the reader, I think, that gets us, that's completely believable in somebody's life—that's why it's startling.

LH We talked about artifice but there is the fact that in poetry you are so often talking to somebody in particular, and that is real and that keeps your feet on the ground. Equally you aren't actually able to talk to the reader. If "my heart melts at the sound of your voice", in 'Desert Phone' there's someone on the phone you love. It's just "phew" and your heart melts. Then you get a letter from them in their handwriting, and it's just "oh".

KC Yes, of course, but there is artifice here all the same, it's a poem. I just think you try and avoid the question by saying you think of it as a sequence of events, but as it is arranged each event defines the stanza or the line, so the poem has nine moments, it is almost ideogrammatic.

LH Ideogrammatic is appropriate since the last one is taken from one of the hexagrams of the *I Ching*.

KC There's a very precise aesthetic it seems to me, although transcribed onto the page as if naively. There's a deal of craftsmanship in this.

LH The way you're putting it makes it sound as though it's very conscious.

KC No I don't think it's conscious, that's why you can't answer it. You wrote it, you can't see it.

LH Ah!

KC I think there's an unconscious answer as well. There are other poems like this that we've looked at before. As the reader you become aware of that line between what's given or what's inspired, or what's made or what's crafted as a result of what's given. Sometimes we're lucky enough to be touched by something that's just given, and I think this might be one of those poems. I know there's somebody on the phone in the desert, but that's a great title anyway—the voice coming out of the desert, the occasion gives it to you, doesn't it? You know, it's just wonderful.

LH It's a real desert. Not some sort of allegorical desert.

KC It has to be a real desert, but that's not the end of its resonance. Here we have the real desert, not just as a literary setting, then it takes on other realities doesn't it? And you've said it's not allegorical—but there are the arid mountains and they also mean something else. There's a sense of distance between these two people, for instance.

LH Yes, there are phones and letters and real events, but also part of it moves in and out of a dream-like series of events.

KC So there's the real desert and a dream desert and what that might mean.

LH And then stepping back from it half way through and saying "How did we get here?", I mean being in this situation as well as being in the desert.

KC The questions accumulate, don't they?

LH Yes.

KC So even this apparently quite plain script taken directly from feeling, the script from the heart, just written onto the page, is also made, there's craft isn't there?

LH As you explain it, yes.

KC I think in other poems too, you slip between styles or different types of discourse as well—in and out of the different worlds in the poems. In the same sense where we begin is not where we end up with poems like 'O, O, O, Northern California'. You know we start with a recognisable world but you kick against that. The reference to business as usual at the end is very ambiguous isn't it?

LH Yes and no. A bit akin to the 'Posters'—'O, O, O, Northern California' sets this exquisite, dream-like life against a wider reality and failure. 'Northern California' is about a self indulgent world—the leisure and luxury and beauty indifferent to what goes on elsewhere. It finishes with a man driving out of town in a car and the radio is playing opera. But you know the dream fades, and ordinary life, earning a living, having responsibilities, all this goes on as usual. You can shut that out for quite a while, but in the end it has to be recognised and dealt with. I think that theme pops up in quite a lot of pieces around this period.

KC Yes, a different reality interrupts the one that's being constructed in the earlier part of the poem.

LH It starts off with all these experiences that are almost too beautiful. Such as "oh rarely fingered jade" and "oh handsome writing book", all these lovely things. In fact they are so exquisite, they are almost in museum cases. They're not part of the real world. This was partly a portrayal of aspects of living in Bolinas. About an hour's ride down the coast was San Francisco with its poverty and its wealth, its violence and its great culture. At least this was a mixed city which had a human balance, whereas this sort of weird oasis of Bolinas, charming and lovely though it was, wasn't real and if it was, it didn't feel right.

KC And the O's at the beginning?

LH An operatic quality.

KC I think this is a pattern we see here also in 'Coat of Arms on the wall in an ancient city' which is interestingly unnamed and unplaced, very unlike 'O, O, O, Northern California' which is very specific to that location and time. 'Coat of Arms on the wall in an ancient city' has a surprising tone. As if, oh here we are, we're going to have a description from a European city. Then the heraldic beasts and the gargoyles seem to trot into the poem and take us into these interesting weekenders in sadomasochism gear. Was it Carnival?

LH No just a normal day.

KC Any old Tuesday then. As before nothing is quite as it seems is it? Tell me something about this poem.

LH It is a very familiar pattern. We see the icon of the Virgin Mary in a church. She just seems to have a look of indifference about the whole thing. She may pity us or she may not even know. So what—tough luck. It's business as usual and things go on while you have all these partings in Venice. You have the boats going through the harbour, dancing bears finishing the day's performances and going home. The bus meets the ferry. The bus drivers are just chatting rather bored. It's putting all the fancifulness into perspective in the wider world. Of course the Doges of Venice stole all of this statuary. The horses on top of St Marks were looted from Constantinople and various other statues have come from various other parts of the world. Some are so eroded by the sea air that people think they're other creatures than what they really are. It's loot. Even the Virgin Mary, this wonderful icon, was stolen from Cyprus by the Venetians in one of their raids or adventures.

KC So things aren't what they seem and things don't belong where they are?

LH Yes.

KC A shifty world here isn't it? There's another example of this but in quite a different way in 'Hand from an Exeter Cloud' where we move from the speaker's dream to a stark recognition of the same moment from outside the speaker's life. Later you think you're in an exhibition of Elizabethan miniatures and undergo a sudden, shocking recognition of seeing a miniature entitled 'Man Clasping a Hand from a Cloud'.

LH I suppose that short cameo of a poem contains quite a lot of the earlier two poems 'O, O, O Northern California' and 'The Coat of Arms'. Again, can I use the word exquisite, art, whether it be a cathedral or Laforgue's poems, is set beside a very human tragedy, the loss of children. And all the art really isn't going to save you when it comes to the essentials.

KC Yes, the guy drives back and goes about his ordinary business in 'Northern California', the bears shuffle off after having done their day of entertainment for the tourists, and here, the stark condition is the recognition of this visionary moment.

LH A kind of stepping aside, double checking. 'Is this something new? asks the clerk sarcastically? Not exactly.' There's the business of hiding in art and it being really no defence when it comes to certain things. This pattern amongst humans is nothing new, people have been doing it for centuries.

KC What interests me in these poems we've just talked about, is that you seem to be peeling back the poem. I think there's a similar process in 'The Heart and Hand, North Road, Brighton', it's only missing the postcode in terms of accurate location. You take a layer off the poem as you proceed, to explore something which appears almost uncontainable in the poem as projected. You start off by writing a Lee Harwood poem and then willfully derail it. You crash the poem so that something new and unexpected seems to jump up. I wonder if the *Mabinogion* reference at the beginning is a clue, as far as the idyll is broken?

LH The poem started with the story of Bran's head, from the *Mabinogion*, in which these people are fine as long as they don't think about the past or of all the horrors. Once they do open the door and let that stuff come in then there's no way they can put it back to the happy time of feasting in the hall. The poem is like a game of leapfrog—one meeting after another and it goes on and ends surprisingly. The Welsh idyll is broken by the admission of past horror. I associated that with seeing the Michael Tippett opera, *King Priam*, which had a grim scene with Achilles bathing his hands in blood.

KC The quotation is "erotic corpse fondling".

LH Yes.

KC A fairly striking notion?

LH It is a very strange, sensual and frightening opera. It had the hair on the back of my neck standing up. So you've got Bran's head and you move to the hacked body of Patroclus and then from that it side steps, a series of side steps, associations, to the idea of Byron clawing Shelley's heart out of a fire, if that was ever true. One thing follows another and suddenly this is interrupted by my running down the street and going into a pub, The Heart and Hand in Brighton, finding a friend and a love scene. Coming out of the opera desperate for a drink, and by accident going into this pub, and by accident this person was there, and stepping in a way into that world of the idyll at the beginning of the story of Bran before they open the door. Put crudely, the poem ends up, despite the horrors of the world, balanced by the love and the tenderness of everyday life, walking along the streets with people, street cleaners brushing the pavements, and it's a very benign world.

KC But you return, in a sense, to the beginning don't you—this quotation at the end "those years the happiest they'd known" and the pun that you play on the name of the pub The Heart and Hand with the line "my heart leaps into your hands".

LH Yes, I guess that's a bit clever.

KC No, I like that. It begins in quite a literary way with the *Mabinogion*, the high art of Michael Tippett—who's perhaps not been taken as an aphrodisiac before, however, and then Byron and Shelley. This is what I mean about stripping it out. The poem becomes more and more literal, the occasion itself takes over.

LH It moves from myths and operas to the very factual. It's set up like prose.

KC Yes, it's in prose paragraphs isn't it? That's what I mean, it's as if you say I'm setting up this artifice, look at this hand and whilst we're watching that hand, I'm actually working with the other hand.

LH Yes.

KC Tricky. Trickster.

LH Brer rabbit.

KC I think it's a key feature in your work.

LH Looking back at it now, I'm still pleased. What I like is taking all these steps which are not expected and suddenly with no intention of going that way but ending up there.

KC But you like side steps and diversions don't you?

LH Yes.

KC It's fresh, fresh as the day. Can we perhaps finish by looking at a longer poem for you, 'The Unfinished Opera for Marian' that comes at the end of *Rope Boy*. Can you just describe the poem for somebody who hasn't read it, what to expect?

LH Well, it is an opera in the sense that it has the plot of an opera, though every so often stepping in and out of it. If you think of the absurdity of most opera plots, say Mozart, it's very difficult to write one which is as mad and illogical as they are. So I wanted to have a go and see if I could write an opera story. That was part of the drive, and also it was writing a poem for Marian, which again is a history of a relationship. These stories are the best way of talking sometimes, like using parables, or like Aesop's fables. It's what we said earlier. It's probably more accurate than you could be just by laying it out naked. I think its very consciously playing games. The poem starts off with an overture which sets a scene in Kansas. This is being seen by a dreamer, and you're being told this by a dreamer. In Act I Scene I the dreamer falls asleep and has a dream, a dream within a dream—it's a like a series of boxes inside boxes. Medieval dream poems are familiar of course and the idea continues right up to Alice in Wonderland.

It starts in Kansas, the home of Dorothy and Oz, and describes the landscape there. It then goes into a more traditional opera setting which is Venice, with all sorts of shenanigans going on. That's Act I Scene I and Scene II, and then III. Then there's an interval in which we step out of the Venetian setting back to Kansas which is more personal, more natural and more contemporary and not playing quite so consciously with the artifice and the props of grand opera. Act II Scene I goes back into the world of opera and then reaches a point where Marianna, the operatic character who is really Marian, enters, and the narrator realises that really the opera is no longer needed and so we drop the curtain on this scene, "I stand in front of the red velvet, the toy theatre, this elaborate allegory of our story." I think it's one of the first times "I" is used other than in the overture. And that goes into a very direct declaration of feeling, away from all the artifice. A declaration of the intensity of love between the I and Marianna/Marian. But at this point you can't just dump all the characters you've created earlier. I mean they're good people, including the Pangolin. While there's this declaration of love going on behind the curtain all the other characters are scuffling their feet, getting very annoyed because they want to continue with the opera. What then happens is that their opera is going to carry on. I don't know what's going to happen but we've got other things to do, so Marian and I, the narrator, just go somewhere else—step sideways.

KC Again.

LH Yes, we step into the wings our arms around each other—the curtain once again opens and the opera continues, and the Pangolin and other characters are doing their bit.

KC And the opera continues not only on stage of course?

LH No, you're right. The strange thing is that, though you've got the very artificial world of opera being portrayed alongside a very intense personal story, if you look at so much opera the basis of it is a very intense personal story.

KC That's what we mean by operatic.

LH In the overture I quote from Massenet's opera *Don Quichotte*. As Don Quichotte lies dying he sings to Sancho Panza, "I promised you an island, now all I can give you is an island of dreams." When I first heard that I had tears in my eyes.

KC You could have written that—that sounds like you.

LH That awful failure. That is a real event. Opera in one way is very, very odd, but equally true to the heart. It directs you back into the world.

KC The opera continues but not only on stage, in the end that link between the elaborate conventions of opera with its stock characters and insistence on strong romantic feeling, even to a quite hysterical pitch—that link isn't broken by the other scene is it? It continues, the two are joined?

LH Yes—though the trappings are slightly different.

KC The undramatic world of Kansas, with Marian sitting on her deck outside her house in Kansas here and now. It doesn't actually make an odd bed fellow with the world of opera at all? Maybe that's the surprising discovery of the poem?

LH Yes.

Walden Pond, 1973:
(l to r) John Wieners,
Lee Harwood,
Lewis Warsh and
William Corbett.

Talking Bab-Ilu

for Anne Stevenson

The words scattered or hidden
since the tower of Babel
and a jealous Jehovah
(get a new job, why don't you?
who needs it? that sort of stuff?).

Up and down the ziggurat stairs,
into the skies into the earth.
A gate for gods, not a confusing babble.
The language of trees, of seas,
of winds, plants, and us beasts.

Music after the flood
in the hills and mountains.
As spring comes a young bull
bellows in a high green field.
You stop and listen.

And the other sounds—
the mew of two buzzards up above,
the drumming of water down
over rock slab over rock slab,
my voice talking to myself.

Listening,   waiting,   drifting
into that space beyond words.
Forgot what I meant to say.
My hands before my eyes.
It can happen.   Clear and bright.

INTERVIEW 5 — FEBRUARY 2008

Nowhere Else

KC My first few questions are about In The Mists: Mountain Poems 1988–1993. A short book but encompassing sharply contrasting experiences. The background reference to Thomas Gray's comment on the mountains, both the horror and the beauty of the mountains, is a clue. How did that book get shaped?

LH I wanted to assemble a collection of my poems to do with the mountains. It's one of the few themed collections I've ever published. The book is in memory of my friend Paul Evans who introduced me to hill-walking and mountaineering and who died in an accident when climbing in the Snowdon Massif in January 1991. Crudely speaking, the book is the before and after of this event, and it has a bridging piece which moves from just the sheer joy of being in the mountains to the loss. It's in praise of being in the hills and it leads to an elegy for Paul Evans. The title itself is, while it's factual, also the title of a piano piece by Janáček which Paul Evans especially loved.

KC So it moves from the beauty to the horror? The grief of that death emerges as the book proceeds, it doesn't overwhelm the book though does it?

LH No. There is grief, as you say, but it's not over the top and melodramatic. That certainly would be an insult to Paul and to what he valued. It would be self-indulgent gush.

KC I think there's a key note in the poetry around this time, a form of accuracy, an almost literal measuring?

LH Yes, it's more precise, it's truer to the facts than any elaboration. There really are certain things that are beyond words, and that poem titled 'For Paul /Coming Out of Winter', ends with the lines:

'How many times we discussed the sea's colours
all beyond description words a mere hint
of what's before our eyes then and now'

You can endlessly discuss the colours, but nothing will do them justice.

KC There are two kinds of poems in the book then, those about the beauty of walking in the mountains and the others about grief? If we take examples of the first kind to begin with 'September Dusk' and 'Visits to the Mountains'. I think they both exemplify those two qualities. They are both stubborn and concerned with specifics, but there's a sense of idyll and of the physical delight of being there. You reject Harwood story-telling for immediacy. In 'September Dusk' it's as if you say, ah but it's not that story. You step away from it.

LH The simple fact was that the facts are far more interesting, far more powerful, in such a landscape than any stories I could make up. The poem 'September Dusk' touches on that indescribable feeling that one has at moments, an amazement at the surrounding world, its colours, its appeal, the taste, the smell of it, the touch of the wind on your skin. Most of all it's the feeling of being totally present. So much of one's consciousness is scattered with thoughts and worries about the future or the past, but actually to be 100% present, in the now, that's an amazing luxury and everything can glow in that condition. Concentration is essential when you're climbing. You can't allow your mind to wander otherwise you're going to have problems, you've got to have your attention in front of you always.

KC So it's an experience of absolute concentration, of attention?

LH Yes, and that attention spreads beyond the actual act of climbing into just looking at everything around you.

KC Is it a doubling of your attention? Attention to the climbing, survival, and an openness that is coming at you from all angles.

LH Yes, and I see them as the same.

KC At the end of 'Visits to the Mountains' you write, 'if you think this is just description, it isn't.'

LH I guess it's, in a way, a rebuke to those who dismiss poetry that has what they call a pastoral rather than an urban setting, as though nature poetry is essentially trivial and 19th century romantic and escapist. The poem is in four sections, all of them describing actual events in the mountains but what they encapsulate is akin to what I mentioned earlier, the attention and amazement. The first one is about climbing in extreme winter conditions and cloud, it's dangerous, but marvellous too.

KC The second type of poem in the book records the loss, as the others record the delight. Taking a lead from 'On The Ledge' and 'For Paul / Coming Out Of Winter', there's a remarkable referential quality in the language, the balanced syntax. They're very finely balanced poems I think. Can you talk about that poise? Were you aware of that at the time, or was it just how it came out?

LH I think I was conscious of it. I had to make it so another person could read it and understand it without being overwhelmed by some gush that was almost so private that it was unreachable. It had to be set in the real world in which the reader also existed.

KC The poems which close the sequence—again there's a poise, there's an acknowledgement rather than any sort of conclusion. It wouldn't be like you to write a conclusion but there's an acknowledgement but in two very different styles. In 'Sandy

Berrigan in Sussex' and 'Chinese Thoughts on Procedure',
I think you're dealing with the same material but in different
ways.

LH 'Sandy Berrigan in Sussex' is an elegy not only for Paul Evans
but also for Sandy's daughter Kate, who was killed in New York
by a hit-and-run driver about the same time. So we both were
trying to live with that, living in this world and savouring its
pleasures as those we've loved would have expected us to. And,
learning how to live with the ghosts in a way that make them like
touchstones for what matters, how we run our lives. 'Chinese
Thoughts' is about just paying attention. The description of
the fox crossing a frozen river, listening out for the cracks. In
Chinese mythology and the *I Ching* that image of the fox is a
symbol of treading carefully, being wary as you move forward.
Foxes are so nervous when they move round, carefully moving
from iceflow to iceflow, to get across the river and listening out
in case the ice is going to crack up. It also reflects the style of
classic Chinese poetry which I love.

KC Right, moving on. *Morning Light*. It must have been written at
the same time but in a quite different work? The subjects are
more varied in *Morning Light*, there are meditative pieces, lyrical
pieces all mixed together, different senses of history—there's
some family history and a bigger political history as well—the
holocaust for instance, the genocide. I wonder what led you off
in these multiple directions?

LH *Morning Light* is a gathering of work written over an 8 year
period and then given a good sieving. I dropped a lot of stuff.
It's certainly a very varied bag.

KC Let me ask you a question about 'African Violets', which is about
your Grandmother, a very direct, moving poem, but again it's
not just about an outpouring of feeling or emotion. In the poem
itself you refer to your own doubts about the poem being equal

to the task as you write it—you question whether you can write it—and also the sense of the world still being out there. Is it possible to talk about technique in a poem like this?

LH Possibly. Early on I say that talking about my grandmother's death is impossible, but somehow I side-step and acknowledge that and carry on. Robert Sheppard told me that this is a tradition in the elegy that goes back centuries. I'm following a familiar pattern in that way, although I wasn't aware of it at the time. And, yes, it is very much concentrated, focused on my relations and feelings for my grandmother Pansy Harwood, but it spreads out to a lot of parallel ideas that were touched on in *In The Mists*, living with the ghosts and then being somehow guided by them.

KC Yes, as an elegy it's full of scenes from the life. Maybe that's the indirectness that makes it so powerful?

LH Most of the poem, once I got over saying I can't write this poem but I will, is various scenes from my memory of her. She's centre stage and she chides me because I say something which is, maybe, a bit emotional. She says, "That was a bit unnecessary, son." She is there saying it.

KC Get on with you and make that rabbit hutch.

LH Earlier you asked about the technique—it just happened, it just flowed.

KC But again it's a poem full of references, full of objects, full of names of things, full of actions.

LH Yes. That produced a far more real and solid tribute and history than any discussion of feeling.

KC 'Dreams of Armenia' is a very different poem, not personal in the same sense. It's obviously a political poem, a political history which is still disputed, the Turkish genocide against the

Armenians. Was that poem brewing up for a long time? There's a good deal of documentation, which suggests research?

LH Well, it took me many years. I became interested in Armenia in the late 1960s through Marian O'Dwyer, who is half-Armenian. At first it was an interest in the music. I had tapes her mother made. It was amazingly moving and beautiful music. Then gradually over the years my interests grew in not just the music but the art, the architecture and then the often tragic history. It was also a parable which had this immense beauty that became the Armenia of my dreams. Because of where Armenia is on a map everybody going east or west to invade elsewhere comes through the front door and out the back door, and the people in between get hammered. I knew I wanted to write about it. I didn't know how. I did a lot of research. A folder full of notes and clippings and I couldn't get it right. I spent five years, 1988–1993, working on this, until finally something clicked and I was able to start the writing. The poem, as I said before, goes beyond Armenia, in fact the beginning is a reflection of how Paul's death often made me like the ancient mariner, continually having to tell the story of his death. There's no denying that one lives with the ghosts and you try to do justice to the life that you're given and which they no longer have. That feeling then continues through my writing about Armenia.

KC Something happened to you which allowed you to write it, prepared you to write it?

LH It was building up and building up, but I knew I could not just write a piece collaging this stuff, making it a poem—it had to be right. It was only when I had done all this research, and got past it. Most of the folder I just had to dump, and then I started almost from scratch. I just moved into it.

KC What strikes me are the different styles and voices incorporated. It isn't just collage. There are quite distinct styles incorporated in the poem? The lyrical, the documentary set side by side? Is that an important technique?

LH Yes that was how I finally cracked how I could write it.

KC Extracting scraps out of documents is easily done, isn't it? It's not just that?

LH I had to include both the facts and then, in that context, the personal. The poets I thought of who use factual history in a poem were Reznikoff in his books like *Testimony* and *Holocaust*, though they're purely the facts rather than the personal. William Carlos Williams' *Paterson* does have the two woven, as does Pound in *The Cantos*. And for me the personal, in amongst all this history, is Marian—our love, our times together and our story. So what happened to Armenia also overshadowed Marian and I take that history personally.

KC The poem is a triumph of that technique. You also introduce a first person presence into the situation, who is clearly not always yourself but is a speaker. Do you see any problems with that?

LH No, not particularly, I'd worked my way into the material, it came that way.

KC Again, to make the point about the mix of this book, if we look at a very different poem 'The Songs of Those Who Are on the Sea of Glass'. Well the title itself is a poem—it's a beautiful phrase. First question, what's the title about?

LH The title is taken from a volume of Welsh hymns by William Williams, who had the bardic name of Pantycelyn, and it was published in 1750 in Welsh. I came across this in a history of Wales and was just so impressed by that title. It seemed to be such a wonderful image, walking across this sea of glass, the surface of it. And also the fact of how precious and rare glass was in the 18th century.

KC It's also an image of mortality isn't it, because the glass might crack and that's the end of your singing?

LH Well the poem is the cardiac poem, I guess, that many poets in their mid-50s get to write.

KC I'd rather not.

LH Not necessarily all. It's a chronicle of being dead and being brought back into what suddenly seemed like an amazing world. Hence Mandelstam, "This earth is a god given palace, the happy heaven . . . the boundless house in which we live our lives." When you come around from all the carvings and anaesthetics you see the sunlight—oh. You've crossed the river and come back again.

KC A celebration?

LH Yes. Earlier when we were talking about Armenia I seemed to be stressing the bleak things. In fact, that poem is more a praise of Armenia and the Armenia I imagine and this too is a song of praise. There's one point where the line comes in "talking in code?". Can anyone understand this if it hasn't happened to them? So you're wondering about writing it, whether anyone could ever do it justice, like for my grandmother.

KC Did you ever think it would be the last poem you wrote?

LH I'm not sure but if it was to be the last thing I wrote, I wanted it to be a song of praise. It wasn't that conscious but if it had been my last poem, I would have been quite happy, especially with the last line.

KC That's about the pyjamas.

LH Yes, "sat up in bed in bizarre pyjamas".

KC Yes, that has your name on it.

LH Yes.

KC Your monogrammed pyjamas.

LH I didn't have any pyjamas before then. I was issued with these at the hospital. They were different colours and faded. One part of the poem comes from years back, I don't know why. I just had a memory of going to Denmark in winter. Waking in the morning, as we approached the Danish coast, to hear the crunching noise of the ship ploughing through the ice-covered sea.

KC The poem itself drops in and out of different levels of awareness doesn't it, the fear coming and going and those returning images, which only later seem to make any sort of sense?

LH And Mr Fox gets in as well—he's in Denmark, "inland a fox trotted nervously across snow-covered fields and streams."

KC In 'Talking Bab–Ilu' you're also writing about your doubt and affirmation as you proceed. There's a similar double take. The mountain landscape is quite clearly itself, but you allow it to suggest something else as well, a first language that we might just sometimes understand—you call us "us beasts", it's a condition that we might recognise. Can you talk about that?

LH That poem does move from fable to the natural world of North Wales. I got interested in the story of the Tower of Babel. Allegedly, in the past, we all talked one language, but the grotesque vanity of the old testament God destroys that because of man's presumption. In fact it's never really said in the Bible why he destroyed the tower and the town is abandoned because the workforce can't communicate anymore. In the poem I suggest we still have one language. The move from fable to the natural world is to show how eventually all our voices speak that one language and that's something we understand.

KC You're suggesting there's something before the individualisation of different languages and different experiences?

LH Yes and the Welsh setting echoes earlier senses of being at one with the world, being totally present.

KC As we were saying at the beginning . . .

LH Yes, being just this one creature in this wild landscape.

KC I think there's a major feature in your work around this time of using a landscape or seascape, using it for what it is, naming it and describing it but also you use it to announce something else. In 'Landscape with Three People', the people are not thinking about the landscape, they're more concerned with their mutual business. Here though the landscape takes on a force, it's more than a setting. I want to come back to this. Happy with that?

LH Yes, there's only one other thing that I could go on about. The Tower of Babel was an exchange with the gods. It's a shared staircase and it wasn't authoritarian. Maybe I'm romanticising this history but I like that sense of equality. It's not an authoritarian system, a God or state. That's why at the beginning of that poem there's an aside. The Tower of Babel tells us about the jealous Jehovah. We want to say to that figure, Jehovah—get a new job, why don't you? who needs it? go get another job—go away somewhere, we don't need you because what's in here is very good, thank you.

Lee Harwood, Chelsea Physic Garden, 1990.

Late journeys

You think you'll sleep so well tonight
warmed with the glow of feeling precious
to someone else out there.   Can it be?

You don't sleep that well,
but what's that simple?
Us animals snuffle around so eagerly.

At dusk—coral pink clouds
lined up along the horizon
like mysterious monuments symbolising "Hope".

A weighty full moon hangs over the pier,
silvers the sea, churns our hearts.
Warm silk summer nights.

The orange lights of provincial railway stations.
People walking home, people taking the last train,
shouting across streets, talking on the platform.

It seems all right
whatever may come.

Genghis Khan's hat

Genghis Khan loves his new mauve hat
sent by a feeble emperor far away.
He wears it all the time,
awake and asleep.

Drums and gongs beaten in the encampment.
Wars and skirmishes in the distance.
Coming and going. Fluttering banners.
Horses kick up dust, flying turf.

Among the tent's yellow silk draperies
we're here.
Mr. Mauve Hat is out,
History is out.

The leaves of summer trees
the look in your eyes.
On a distant steppe now
a threadbare hat lying in coarse grass.

INTERVIEW 6 — FEBRUARY 2008

Courage, traveller.

KC Over these interviews we've touched upon forty-odd years of writing. In all that time you've been writing poetry and you've translated Tzara but never any other sort of writing. Why's that?

LH With academic work and journalism, and even reviewing, I have no talent for such work nor the confidence. The few times I have written critical pieces they are always in praise of somebody whom I really like a lot, like James Schuyler. Those pieces involve such a lot of work, far more than it takes to write a poem. I just haven't got the time to do it.

KC You'd rather write a poem.

LH Yes, I would.

KC The work of others is involved in your work too, there have been different collaborations and we've spoken about them. Have there been times when you've not written much or you've written nothing at all?

LH After the *Collected* came out I didn't write anything for a year and a half, I was frozen by it. I just thought what can I do now? It's only going to be a repeat. Some writers do have formulas, a practice like writing every day, and maybe it works for them, I guess it does work for them but I've never been able to do that. I just wait and live my usual life, read a lot, go to exhibitions, poetry readings to find out what other people are doing, go on walks in the hills, etc, etc, and talk to friends. The talk with friends is especially a source of writing, of ideas, for me.

KC Don't push it, just carry on?

LH Yes there are various pieces of writing that really show that they're being written because a person desperately needs to write rather than the actual work having a necessity behind it. I'm thinking about a poet who I admire greatly, Paul Blackburn. He wrote a book called *In the City*. It's all about living on the Lower East Side in New York and travelling on the subway, the people sitting around him, and so on. Eventually in his later years he had a position in up state New York as a writer in residence at a university, and the poems just lose it. It's as though the poems are "well, I'm sitting in this room and looking out on the lawns and trees with a blank piece of paper and I'm a writer in residence and I guess I'd better write", that's about it!

KC Neglect is easier to live with isn't it?

LH Yes.

KC So over those decades of writing some things must have come more readily than others and maybe you've written at different paces as well? Do you write slower now than you did or faster?

LH I'm not aware of a pattern but I think that I do take longer now, especially compared with what I wrote in the 60s where sometimes I'd write a poem in a day. In the last year I've written three poems and each poem has taken me about 7 or 8 months. You've still only got a page of poetry, and maybe a reader won't be able to tell the difference between that and something written in the 60s, but I am slower.

KC Let me pursue this. Yesterday we spoke about 'The Songs of Those Who Are on the Sea of Glass', which is as fresh as anything. How long did it take to write that?

LH I'm not sure, but I would imagine a couple of months. I think in your early work you have this drive and confidence, and then later on you're looking more carefully, possibly, to get the words right, to not allow any foolishness, to make it just right—fine tuned. Not over tuned, but . . .

KC I was wondering also how do poems begin for you? A lot of your work begins with a picture, or a painting, a postcard, it's ekphrasis isn't it? But that's not the only type of prompt. I just wonder if there's a typical way you go about writing a poem?

LH I'm not aware of a typical way. It is as though the poem almost starts assembling itself, then I step in. The poems are usually, with exceptions, written without an intention—it's afterward I realise what's happened in the poem. You develop it and work it so that it's clearer. Sometimes it's as though writing is almost a matter of instinct rather than conscious planning. In Cocteau's film *Orphée*, Orphée is dictated poems over the radio and he just transcribes them. Jack Spicer says similar things "a poet is a radio". The poems are in the atmosphere and you are just the receiver that captures them and sometimes reception isn't so good but it does get through. As far as what sparks it beside paintings, it can be a conversation with a friend, or a film, or some phrase overheard when you're walking down the street. I did a set of six poems called 'Gifts Received' which was in a way my way of getting out of that block after the *Collected* and each of the six is sparked by a gift from a friend. The first one is Anne Stevenson telling me a line she'd had in a dream, and then another one is a line actually taken from a poem by Ian Davidson, another one is an Italian fruit wrapper, which you gave me, another is a Mexican bus ticket.

KC There can be just the chance event too. I'm thinking of that late poem where the girls are tripping down this street out here.

LH Yes.

KC That's in the beginning of 'Take a Card'.

LH It starts with a very bleak winter setting and then these young girls are going down to check out wedding dresses—you know, life goes on, lots of things are happening despite what seems a bleak scene.

KC When you get into the swing of something, do you think "oh yes, this is me, this is how I do it"? I know you're a note-taker.

LH I have notebooks and I use them a lot.

KC And over the years, I should imagine, you'd have kept them?

LH Yes. And, because I have a very bad memory, I also use a commonplace book in which I copy out bits of poems or books that I like a lot, so I know I can go back and find them. But the notes, sometimes, they can be the start of a poem. It may be just a thought that comes into my head when I'm on the train. It's very useful.

KC And do you go back to them and use them? Do you ever go back and look over old copies?

LH Now and then, but usually something is in the notebook that I think has possibilities. I copy it out again into my writing book and then it really is getting seriously lined up for a poem. Sometimes, like this piece I'm trying to write now, I'm not quite sure where it's going to go. I put odd jottings down and I know that one morning it'll be clear and I'll start and once I've got going, hopefully, it'll be all right.

KC Very orderly habits then. Well, it's commendable. Let's move onto some particular poems. Looking at the most recent work, I want to go back to those terms that Robert Sheppard uses, about the combination of the near and the far and the sense of intimacy and distance, "distanced and intimate" were the terms he used. Let's look at this idea in three poems. 'Late Journeys' from the same book, 'Genghis Khan's Hat' and 'The Silk Veil' because you explore those two experiences in different ways. In 'Late Journeys' for instance there's a voice that I would recognise because of the tone, the nearness of the experience, the domestic setting and the tenderness of it. What do you think? Let's talk about the way you do that.

LH I think 'Late Journeys' is fairly clearly the sort of persona that comes through in a lot of my work. There is really only one voice in that poem.

KC And it's very quiet, isn't it? Word by word quiet.

LH Yes, it's a personal statement but it's also insisting on putting the statement in context.

KC You're such a damned optimist aren't you?

LH Yes.

KC Like the last, you know the last two short lines "it seems all right/ whatever may come".

LH Yes.

KC That's a signal note for you.

LH Mr Perky.

KC Yes, Mr Perky sometimes—up and about in the morning.

LH I worked for the railways and that's my one railway poem. It was about bringing in trains late at night, those orange lights in small stations and one or two people standing around.

KC Yes, it's like a Cornell box, there's a comforting exactness about it. It's almost like a model of itself. One of my favourite poems by you is 'Genghis Khan's Hat'. Here we have the historical figure treated to satire, his hat ends up rolling in the dry grass, so this mighty conqueror becomes an object of derision, his remoteness shrunk?

LH It's a parable of sorts. You've got this story of Genghis Khan and his camp and all the action. In amongst his going off on his adventures the narrator and his lover are inside this silken tent. Inside we have their love and outside Genghis Khan is going off to do things. Eventually his magnificent hat will be found lying in the grass somewhere, but meanwhile back at the tent there's this almost timeless moment of intimacy. Also the little subtext is the fact that it involves a children's story. One of my kids when they were young had a book at school for learning how to read called *The Village with Four Corners* and there was Mr Green Hat, Mr Red Hat, Mr Blue Hat and Mr Yellow Hat and so the children learned their colours. Genghis Khan became Mr Mauve Hat.

KC Mr Mauve Hat is out, history is out, in this poem history is out. In other poems it's not, for instance 'Dreams of Armenia', and going back to the very beginning to 'Cable Street', history is very much in.

LH Yes, that's true. This is a self-indulgent moment, it's just this one moment, the lovers' sensual pleasure.

KC Yes, who's scared of Genghis Khan anyway? That threadbare hat lying in coarse grass. Following this line of argument then, we've gone from the intimacy of 'Late Journeys' to a more remote figure Genghis Khan made small. There's an interesting confusion of the near and far in 'The silk veil'. Why is it called that?

LH I think it's an image of sensual pleasure and immediacy. I was thinking of the feel of silk, a sort of silken world. You know, I don't think silk actually occurs in the poem.

KC What interests me is the figure of the migrating tribe. They are in transit and somehow they're transformed into a fountain that swells up with dark water, or that might just be a scene in the city, and then they settle, stop travelling. Then we have industrial

105

scenery, which is followed by consideration of the darkness of your lover's hair—the focus becomes sharper and sharper and smaller and smaller. A curious journey.

LH A similar pattern to 'Genghis Khan's Hat'. There's quite a series of elaborate stories leading through.

KC A transformation.

LH Ending up with the intimacy. In terms of sources the beginning of this is sparked by a place called Goodwood Sculpture Park in Sussex. They had this group of figures, human figures, life-size, coming out of a wood and they just were stood there—it was an amazing sight. I took it on from there. They almost fade into the dusk, and then you have this fountain swelling, and then the night, and then on to a frosty, rosy dawn.

KC And all of this happens without any fuss—there's no self importance in that series of transformations.

LH No, it doesn't need it. You have this strange ghostly tribe and the fountains with leaves swirling around underneath the surface, and then it's like meanwhile there are also factories, offices and backyard repair shops in the world.

KC Can we talk about another set of three poems which are connected—'Salt Water', 'Pagham Harbour Spring', and 'Cwm Nantcol'. This is my question about how you use landscape. 'Salt Water' again is a very tender poem where there's a connection between the submarine seascape, the underwater world, and the child. There are moments of absolute directness and also of indirect attention, to allow the metaphor to do its work as well. Can you talk about that poem?

LH I found this special new section of Kew Gardens where they have all the plants growing under the sea. There are tanks, a North Atlantic tank, or a Pacific Ocean tank, with the sort of plants that will grow there, plus the creatures and the fish, so it's the full picture. It was just breathtaking to see it—it was amazing. You have that wonderment and I was equally thinking how my daughter Joey would have enjoyed it. You looked at this as a child. Everything stops and your attention is completely focused on something whether it be a butterfly or a fish in a tank. I'm talking about the complexity and beauty of this world and it is quite a complex world if you study the structure of coral reefs. It's not all smiley, creatures are preying on other creatures. The poem shifts back and forth, from the picture of the underwater world and then back to reality, which is the hospital building where my daughter was then. She only lived for three days. There's an intense scene, intense wonderment and also I guess intense grief realising how this child would be so delighted by the world, whether it be the fish in the coral reef or what's happening in the town. At the end there's an image of the sea again and the phosphorous trail behind a ship and my looking up the origin of the word "phosphorous" and finding out it meant "light bringing". That seemed like a symbol of joy, and of her.

KC Yes, hence the final line of the poem.

LH Yes.

KC In 'Pagham Harbour Spring', which in some ways is a simpler poem I think, we have the scene described, and there is a sense of absorption in each moment of the scene. But then again you speak to your daughter?

LH 'Pagham Harbour Spring' is a simpler version of 'Salt Water'. It's not moving into a collage of information about the undersea world, it's just the landscape at Pagham Harbour. It ends with how she would have loved these particulars and the particulars are not only Pagham Harbour. There's a railway track nearby and there's a man, pushing a refreshments trolley along the train's aisle, whose shirt is beautifully ironed and his waistcoat is very neat. This working man is showing care and attention to what he does. It's just, as they would say today, an accessible version of the poem, 'Salt Water'.

KC As we would say today. And you've done the thing you do, which is the world is made almost like a Cornell box, there's a model quality to it, because of the precision of each moment.

LH It wasn't intentional but looking back I realise, yes, I'm building a landscape, starting with the light as a summer's day starts and then the scent of the gorse, then the birds, then the train passing by, and my daughter Joey being in the poem. It finishes up with how much she would appreciate "the children running on the dyke bank, / absorbed in this world". It's what we said earlier, the ghosts in a way give us necessary reminders of what matters.

KC 'Cwm Nantcol' is a particular landscape and I think in that poem you're carrying on your argument about the pastoral.

LH That's true.

KC Explain that to me.

LH It's a poem in three sections and it starts with a straight description of 'Cwm Nantcol', which is a valley near Llanbedr that I go to a lot. I've been trying for years to describe this landscape. It's very difficult to do it justice but what happens is a double story in the way I've described the landscape and then question why this place fascinates me. Why do I need to return to this place again and again? It's like some sort of comfort and a sense of timelessness one gets in this mountain landscape. The second part is an account of a Polish officer who after the end of the Second World War was stationed in Britain with the Polish Army. He was the father of the painter Andrzej Jackowski. Wherever he was stationed, in these crumbling army camps, he would make a garden. It would be almost like a miniature Poland because he would always have the same vegetables, the same flowers. He would create home wherever he was. I realised that somehow this landscape is akin to the need people have to feel at home. I'm using the words "at home" in a lose sense. The third part of the poem returns to the Welsh landscape and admits that okay there's the city, but this place, this valley, still fascinates me.

KC So that argument with some of our stricter brothers and sisters, who would regard the pastoral as a piece of sentimental and poetic indulgence, is that psychologically it's more significant than that and also it's still involved with the world anyway— here is history.

LH Yes, it's not in any sense an escape. This landscape is not an invention of Georgian poets of the '20s. It's a real place and the rocks are there and the trees are there. Just as the Polish garden was real. You can't deny it, it's just factual, and okay there is a city. Most of us do live in an urban setting, we have to survive, but that doesn't mean you can deny what's outside the cities or that that hasn't got an immense presence in our lives.

KC And that reality is there in terms of the particular history of the landscape and also in the sense of the city as still present—but it allows what you want, stillness beyond words?

LH Yes in the actual valley, although it gives you a sense of stillness, there are the rocks clawed by a glacier from the Ice Age, and now on these rocks there are plants and moss. It's not stagnant, there's a history unfolding. The timescale may be different but . . .

KC Yes. I said three poems about your use of landscape. Can I add another? 'The Wind Rises'. I think you do something else there with landscape.

LH It's not an imaginary landscape but one built on visits to the Czech Republic and Northern California and in Britain. And, it's influenced very much by a CD by Istvan Martha called *The Wind Rises* where he collages his music with the sound of a dog barking on the edge of a square, a village jazz band playing on the street, a helicopter flying overhead, the sound of a distant sawmill. This collage of the world in provincial Hungary I found to be a fantastic, beautiful work. It's like the film *Il Postino* where the main character and the regular postman go round tape-recording all the noises of the island—the sea, the wind in the bushes, and so on. I just thought "God, if I could write a poem that good"—it would be so vivid, it would be wonderful. This poem is also a lot to do with getting older and what we've talked of, the ghosts you have to live with.

KC You say, ". . . the ghosts are with us. We live with them, that loss."

LH Yes. There are other aspects in this poem too. There is a wintry scene, village life, people are going about their occupations. The noise of the factories, somebody sweeping a gutter and also Sandy Berrigan sweeping the houses of rich people in California.

KC You've mixed several landscapes from different real places but also there's an element of allegory, of the frozen landscape.

LH Yes, that's akin to age. And the very last line about the "golden gown" is a reflection of an old Hungarian folk song. The young man always has to leave to make his fortune because he can't get enough wealth together at home to marry the woman. So he's going to go to America or wherever to make money and send back a golden gown to her for them to get married. And, of course, as so often happens, he never does, the golden gown never comes.

KC Landscape then is a major device, and you're stepping in and out of that landscape, as we talked earlier about you stepping in and out of artifice as well.

LH Yes.

KC It's a technique, I think, that becomes more and more apparent in your later work as well.

LH Yes, I think, it's more reflective. I don't know. The more you write the more you have a sense of how difficult and nearly impossible it is to say these things.

KC To be satisfied with what you're writing?

LH Yes. Zbigniew Herbert ends one of his Mr Cogito poems, "he would like to remain faithful / to uncertain clarity."

KC Ah, that's pretty much on the nail. But actually at the same time, you seem more at ease with the multiplicity of these poems, with using that landscape in several different ways.

LH I suppose because of my feeling that this is in a way a more accurate representation of how the world works as opposed to how one would like it to work.

KC Can we look at some of the pieces in 'Take a Card', more recent work. It seems to me in this collection there are two very strong feelings. One is that you are aware of time passing but also that you refuse elegy. Each poem is like the picture you want on the wall.

LH Yes.

KC The icons on the iconostasis. As you say 'the objects we choose to hang or pin on our walls' and the moods change and subjects themselves are quite varied—"girls tripping down the street to buy a wedding dress", your Uncle's citation, and ever present orchids, as well. Am I on the right lines here? You're saying no, there is no completion aren't you, no final word?

LH Yes because there never is. I love that essay by Carlos Fuentes on Diderot, where he says, "The novel both reflects and creates an unfinished world made by men and women who are also unfinished. Neither the world nor its inhabitants have said their last word." And so I enjoyed assembling this collage of unfinished material. I wanted to have that freedom to sling in this bag all these different things which I know are different, but equally somehow, a bit like *Dream Quilt*, make a whole.

KC Hence the idea of a pack of cards that you can shuffle and play in different hands?

LH Originally the idea was the whole set of 52 pieces would be printed on cards. They would be unbound and you could read the poem how you wanted to. You could shuffle the cards and follow a different reading. In fact, there are only 26 of them. The remaining 26 of them have to be made by somebody else. The idea of shuffling them was there when I wrote them. It gave me a marvellous sense of freedom. It doesn't matter that it's left unfinished, finished doesn't exist.

KC So no thank you to the elegy then? You're not writing any final conclusion?

LH No, not for myself anyway!

KC Here's a quotation I found from the British sculptor Lynn Chadwick, I'm hesitating to say to end with. He had a working life of about 50 years, bashing metal artfully, and he said at the end of that time, "I always feel I'm only just starting, just learning how to do it." What would you say to that? It sounds like you.

LH I would say that is very true and is a very necessary approach for any artist no matter what they do.

KC Okay, we're done. Did you burn the ricks?

LH No, I didn't.

KC Innocent m'lud.

Printed in the United Kingdom
by Lightning Source UK Ltd.
130330UK00001B/85-111/P